To We The People

TO WE THE PEOPLE

Sixty-three Petitions
That Will Heal America

Christopher Ben Largey

Copyright © 2009 by Christopher Ben Largey.

Library of Congress Control Number: 2009906366
ISBN: Hardcover   978-1-4415-4944-0
             Softcover   978-1-4415-4943-3

All rights reserved. No part of this book may be reproduced or transmitted in any form or by any means, electronic or mechanical, including photocopying, recording, or by any information storage and retrieval system, without permission in writing from the copyright owner.

For information about permission to reproduce selections from this book, Wright to Permission, at Christopher Largey
**270 E. Hunt Highway Suite 16 #224
San Tan Valley AZ 85143**

This book was printed in the United States of America.

To order additional copies of this book, contact:
Xlibris Corporation
1-888-795-4274
www.Xlibris.com
Orders@Xlibris.com

CONTENTS

Acknowledgments 9
Preface 11

Hunger 15
The Federal Drug Administration and Another Piece Of Paper 17
Ulterior Motives and the President of the United States 18
The Oath and the Lie 20
The Deficit 23
Insurance and the Leech 29
Consumer Reports 34
Article II, Section 4 36
Judges 40
Heroes 42
Crime and the Prison System 44
Aggregate, the Hammer, and the Illegal 47
Brownie Points, Lawyers, and The Insurance Companies 52
Community Service 55
Taxes 56
Money Down the Drain And Fixing Things That Aren't Broken 58
Iraq War for Sale 60
Perjury, Adultery, and Sex 64
Thirty-Eight Million 69
God is I Am 74
Welfare is not fair 76
Blah, Blah, Blah, and Your Vote 77
The Draft 81
Presidential Executive Orders 82

My Mission Statement 87

DEDICATION

I dedicate this book to love. For it was love that created this world, and it was that same love that our forefathers had, who wanted to have a better life for everyone. And it was that same love that my mother showed toward me when she raised me from a child to an adult.

    Yeah, I dedicate this book to love.
Laus Deo

Acknowledgments

A thank you goes out to my sister Sue who influenced part of this book; the man who gave me the idea about putting big business on the postage stamp; the man who elaborated on prisoners working in the fields; my friend Mickey who reminded me what a Christian was; Koinonia House; *Wikipedia*, the free encyclopedia; the *Iraq War For Sale* video; The movie Sicko and everyone else who had a part in influencing my life.

Preface

When I was just two and a half years old, there was this man who gave a speech on the steps of the Washington Monument before more than two hundred thousand people. I mention him because he stands for the same things that I want to get all Americans to do, and that is strive, to be the very best that we can all be. That man was Martin Luther King, Jr., and he had a dream; I would like to make his dream become a reality.

I can quote many famous people all day long; however, I choose to quote only one person, and it's Martin Luther King, Jr. He said, "The day our lives begin to end is when we become silent about things that matter."

I pray that all of you who read these writings will get involved and care about what is right.

I wrote this book in hopes of uniting all of *We The People* in a last-ditch hope that we indeed can fix all the wrong that is wrong with this, the greatest country in the world.

Notice the title *To We The People*. Well, that's you and it's your friends, family members, even the people you don't like. It's all of us except those in our country who want to keep this nation of ours from thriving.

More than likely, it's the ones who, if you really must know, are the people who we put into office. They have allowed corporate America to dictate policies, all because of the all-powerful god, the dollar.

Our government is run by greed. You and I know it's true, but here's the good news: it's all about to change, all because you're going to do something about it, isn't that great? I'm going to get you to *vote*.

I remember growing up leaving our keys in the car, leaving our front door unlocked, and being able to sleep when we went to sleep at night with not a care of any harm coming to us in any way. It can be that way again.

I remember our teachers, saying that the biggest problems that they were facing each day were no homework being turned in on time and the chewing of gum.

Do you wish that we could get back to those days, living a carefree life and not worrying about who may be hiding in the back of your car waiting to cause you harm? I know we can if we all vote that we want that kind of life again.

You see, there are more good people in this, the greatest country in the world, than bad, and I think that if we *all* decide together to change the things that are wrong, we can have that life again.

But we all must come together, or shall I say that we must all become united for the first time since our forefathers started this, the greatest country in the world.

In this book you will see how, with a few changes being made by our employees and the government, we will be able to end hunger, end welfare, pay off the deficit, and make our judges become accountable for their actions for the first time. I'll show you how we can lower our taxes and much more.

I'll show how, if we all decide to do just one thing, we can fix all the things that are wrong with this, the greatest country in the world, and that one thing is called *voting*. If we all do that one thing, I'll show you some grateful children out there who will grow up saying what a great job all of *We The People* did for their future.

This is a brief lesson on what happens to a country when it is near or over two hundred years old.

All countries start off about the same. First, people get tired of *bondage* and want a new country. Next is *great courage* getting up the nerve to do something about it; then comes *liberty*, and a new country is born. The next thing to happen is *abundance*: "Oh my gosh, there is so much of everything. Isn't this great!" Then comes *complacency*, and that's where all the problems start. Now, I'm not sure when this took place in our country, but I guess it was when the discovery of oil and what oil could do for us happened. Next is *apathy*, which is a state of *indifference*, you know, when you suppress emotions such as *concern, excitement, motivation,* and *passion*. An apathetic individual has an absence of interest or concern for emotional, social, or physical life. They may also exhibit an insensibility or sluggishness.

Often, apathy has been felt after witnessing horrific acts such as the killing or maiming of people or when a government abuses its power for their own gain, and the apathetic person just doesn't care. That person may think, "Don't bother me. I have a house and a car, my kids are doing great in school, I'm making a good living, and my spouse loves me, so don't buck the system. Everything is fine. Just leave me alone."

Then another one that is bad comes next, and that is *dependence*. I wonder how many people in our country right now depend on our government to take care of them. Obviously, it's at an all-time high right now. Guess what's next? It's the last of what happens to a country just before it becomes a new country again, and that's *bondage*. Can you guess where our country is right now?

It's time we all started caring for this country by getting involved and doing that one thing: *vote*!

If you really care for the ones who came before you, the ones who gave their lives for your freedom, then vote. At the back of this book are the petitions that we need all of you to sign and send in so we can heal this the greatest country in the world. If not, please, with my support, please pack your stuff and leave this, the greatest country in the world. Thank you.

Chapter One

Hunger

Hunger is a terrible thing, but do you know what's worse? Being able to do something about it and not doing it.

I think that everyone in this country has, at some point in their lives, been hungry at one point or another, some more than others, and sometimes people will do whatever it takes to feed their own. I know that I would.

There was this woman who, for whatever reason, was in financial trouble, went into a supermarket to steal food to feed her children and got caught. She got arrested, and they took her children away, all because of a piece of paper and some ink.

Restaurants throw enough good food away, food that can feed the hungry in every city in every state in the United States every day. Are we not able to feed the hungry because of one law that says we can't do it? You mean because of some words on a piece of paper, the hungry will remain hungry and, in some cases, die because of malnutrition?

I don't know. I think a few lives being taken from hunger is worth the ability to say, "I have a piece of paper that says no one can eat of the food that they were going to throw away because they didn't sell it."

I wonder how many people to date have died and have gone to jail since someone in the government made this paper become a reality.

This first petition that we need to sign is the one that will feed all the hungry in this, the greatest country in the world.

Rumor has it that the restaurants could get sued if someone eating their food gets sick; thus, let's not do it because of that reason.

Well then, we should allow people to be able to sign away their rights so they can eat. Is that what it would take for that law to change?

They say that you can't sign away your rights because of some other piece of paper which says you can't. Our employees, the government, do it all the time to better their own needs. Why can't their bosses, *We The People*, have that same choice? When you sign up in the military, you become property of the U.S. government. If you go out and get sunburned from laying out at the beach or pool, the government can do some not-so-nice things to you because you have damaged government property.

You signed away your rights for that. Why can't you do it for other things as well? If right now a piece of paper says that we can't do it, can't we just replace it with one that says that we can? Can it be that easy? I think so!

Is that what it will take to feed the hungry—another piece of paper that says they can? Because if that's all, I'll give them one of mine, or they can do their jobs. I mean, after all, isn't that why we put them into office, to take care of us?

I think that a few of our employees need to lose their jobs because they suck at them. Think about it just for a second: they can walk on the moon, but we have hunger in our country. What will it take for them to eat of the food they throw away?

Will it take you to vote for that to happen? Which one do you think will work? I wonder—if *We The People, all of us,* told our employees to do this for us, would they? Are we really the bosses, or are they? If *We The People* are, what if we vote for the hungry not to be hungry anymore? What say you?

Almost the last question: why haven't our employees fixed this problem of hunger? It seems to me that of all the problems we face, this solution to that problem is an easy one. Okay, last question: since this is an easy problem to fix, why haven't they done it? Makes you wonder, hummmmm, makes you wonder what other things that are wrong that they can so easily fix that they don't. *Humm.*

Chapter Two

The Federal Drug Administration and Another Piece Of Paper

Rumor has it that the major shareholders in the pharmaceutical companies are the leaders of the FDA. Do you see a problem with this?

Do you understand what this means? It means that the ones who get to say which drugs will help us in time of need will profit from it.

This next petition might very well just save your life. Is it right that the ones that we put into power get to tell us if we live or not? Because as of right now, that's the way it is.

Some people are dying from incurable diseases. Then someone comes up with a treatment that can possibly cure them, and the FDA says no.

Is this just another piece of paper? Or is it this time a money issue? Someone comes up with a possible cure for, let's say, cancer, and all you have to do is take one pill and you're cured. Then the FDA says no to the drug that heals you, all because they will lose money not being able to sell all the other drugs that help you get through the disease. They say that they will lose billions if they allow this new pill to hit the market. Should we pass a law that makes sure that things like this don't happen ever again? Is it fair that our employees get to tell us that we are going to die all because they want to make money, or is it because of another piece of paper?

Don't you think we should take away the pieces of paper that take away from our livelihood? Should we not give people the choice to make their own decisions about how we live? I know that if I was dying and someone possibly had a cure, I would sign away my rights to not come after them if the treatment caused me harm. Hey, I'm dying anyway—right? Again, if the government can do it, why can't we? *We The People* should also make sure that no member of the FDA has shares in any of the pharmaceutical companies, and also we should make sure that if someone has a possible cure, they have a right to offer it to us.

If we all vote for this to happen, do you think that our employees will do it for us? Well, what do you think? Will you vote and let us know?

Chapter Three

Ulterior Motives and the President of the United States

I don't think that when our forefathers wrote the constitution they knew it would govern three hundred million people. I don't think they could have, and I do think that if they knew what our government has done with what they came up with—well, I think they'd turn over in their graves.

Our forefathers all got together and made up the rules by which everyone was equal and everyone had the same opportunities as everyone else. They wanted a better place to live away from tyranny. They made up these rules because they cared.

I mean, they really cared. They gave of themselves to better other people. Well, I don't know about you, but those are the kind of people I want running my country. The ones that care about their job, that care for people. I want the ones that will give of themselves for the sake of others, someone to look out for me and watch my back in case someone wants to harm me. I want my forefathers back.

I want a government of people who are *We The People*, that will do their jobs and nothing else, not groups of people who have hidden agendas and want a job to better them. You know it's true. They spend thirty million dollars on a campaign to get elected to an office that only pays eighty thousand dollars a year. Hum, I wonder why.

The government that we have now is driven by greed. Politicians think, "How much money can I get no matter who suffers?" I bet we have lots of pieces of paper that were drafted up just for that very purpose.

I want a president who will do his job, take charge of his duties, and see them fulfilled. I want a president who will be just like me, perfect. The perfect president is one who will never give up trying to make things better in all areas and not stop until victory is reached. What a great *goal*.

I'm far from perfect with the exception of one area of my life, and that is my will to try to make things better for all people, even at the cost of giving my life to prove it.

It's one thing to say that you're satisfied with your efforts in how you run your business and that you don't want to make it grow any larger, but as president of the United States you don't have that luxury. You must at all times be concerned with the welfare of your people.

I'm not sure of the date and length of time, but President Bush Jr. spent somewhere around one to three months at his ranch in Texas, not in his oval office taking care of business. You can't do that. Oh my gosh, how dare he do that when three hundred million people depend on him to do his job daily? There is too much that has to be done for him to do that. If I were your president, I would be there every day, with the exception of holidays and vacations, until we reached our goal of uniting all people and fixing all the problems that we have now.

I think that all the presidents of the past, at least the ones that I have seen take office, lied when they took the oath of office to "faithfully execute the office of the President of the United States and [. . .] to the best of [their] ability, preserve, protect and defend the Constitution of the United States."

I say they lied because, in my opinion, they had ulterior motives. They didn't seek the presidency the way our forefathers did. Come on, think about it.

If they did, then they would hire people who would judge people fairly. They would make sure that they would not pervert justice or show partiality. They would not accept bribes and follow justice alone so that all of *We The People* could live in peace.

Do you think that if all the people in office were to do their jobs and be guided by those rules, at least half of the problems we have now wouldn't be problems anymore? Like I talked about earlier, corporate America is the reason all presidents and the like signed up with ulterior motive: *money*.

Chapter Four

The Oath and the Lie

This petition, if signed, will scare the something out of our members of Congress.

Hey, can you tell the difference between the two?

Congress can't because if they did, they wouldn't commit these crimes unless they were sure you wouldn't do anything about them. Sounds about right, doesn't it?

So maybe if given the opportunity that we would do something about it, they would not commit them. But what should we do, and whom do we call?

I know, we call our congressmen and tell them. But wait, that doesn't work because they won't take your call, they're too busy. According to the constitution, for every thirty thousand citizens there should be one representative. If we had one for every thirty thousand, then our country would run smoother, all because we could voice our opinions and concerns to our representatives. Then they, in turn, would bring them up to the proper authorities.

The way it is now is there are 535 members of Congress. Divide that by the number of the population, and that works out to be one representative for every 56,074,766 people. No wonder this country of ours is in the shape it's in. How can they possibility hear from the ones who have a complaint or suggestion? They can't.

Do you know the definition of the word "oath"?

An *oath* is either a promise or a statement of fact calling upon something or someone that the oath-maker considers sacred, usually a god, as a witness to the binding nature of the promise or the truth of the statement of fact. To swear is to take an oath. You know, "I swear to tell the truth the whole truth and nothing but the truth, so help me God."

A person taking an oath indicates this in a number of ways. The most usual is the explicit "I swear," but any statement or promise that includes "as my witness" or "so help me" with being something or someone the oath-taker holds sacred is an oath. Many people take an oath by raising their right hand

and placing their other hand on the Holy Bible, thus indicating the sacred witness through their action.

Okay, in other words, their oath is their bond, and when making an oath, they will never sway from the truth. If they said it they meant it; you could go to the bank with their word. It's that strong of a language.

The people who swore an oath to protect us, the ones who we have entrusted with our future, I believe most of them all lied because if they didn't, our country would be a better place than it is right now.

Did you know that all senators and representatives, the members of the several state legislatures, and all executive and judicial officers, both of the United States and of the several states, shall be bound by oath or affirmation to support this constitution?

The oath of office is something that all people who decide that they want to run this country of ours must do.

An *oath of office* is an oath or affirmation a person takes before undertaking the duties of an office, usually a position in government or within a religious body. The laws of the state, religious body, or other organization often require such oaths before the person may actually exercise the powers of the office or any religious body.

Some oaths of office are a statement of loyalty to a constitution or other legal text or to a person or other office-holder (e.g., an oath to support the constitution of the state or of loyalty to the king.) Under the laws of a state it may be considered *treason or a high crime* to betray a sworn oath of office.

Wow, I guess if you take an oath to do your job and then you decide to do other things with your position of office, you can go to jail for not doing your job. That couldn't be happening, could it? I mean, they put their hand on a Bible and swore to God that they would not fail at their responsibility to us.

For other officials, including members of Congress, it specifies they "shall be bound by Oath or Affirmation to support this constitution."

> *I do solemnly swear (or affirm) that I will support and defend the Constitution of the United States against all enemies, foreign and domestic; that I will bear true faith and allegiance to the same; that I take this obligation freely, without any mental reservation or purpose of evasion; and that I will well and faithfully discharge the duties of the office on which I am about to enter.*

"So help me God."
When is enough?
We need to send them a message that
enough is enough.

If you don't start doing your job
then we will invoke
article 2 section 4 of the constitution.

There might, as of right now, be over 450 of the 535 members of Congress that are eligible for impeachment.
Imagine that.

Chapter Five

The Deficit
Or
13,000,000,000,000
That's a big number, isn't it?
Thirteen trillion dollars!

I think that you do not understand just how big that number really is, so I will put it in terms that you will understand. But before I do, I will give you a history lesson first.

It took our country over two hundred years of being the United States to get to a five trillion dollar deficit. It took the Bush administration just eight short years to double it to ten trillion, and now the Obama administration has added three trillion to it in just his few short months in office.

Okay, here is how much thirteen trillion really is. You will have to pay *three hundred fifty-six million one hundred sixty-four thousand three hundred and eighty-three dollars* a day for the next **100 Years** to pay it off. *Big number isn't it!*

If we do not stop this kind of irresponsible spending the people in the know believe that within the next 10 years that our government will add another 10 trillion to our deficit, then we as or should I say that your great or great great grand children will have to earn 630,136,986 a day to pay it off. It needs to end now, or else!!!

Do you know how much money a congressman gets when he retires from active service? He retains his full pay until he dies. Did you know that all he has to do is complete one full term of service to get that retirement?

Guess what happens to his salary when he dies? It goes to his children, and they get to receive his retirement salary. Then, when they die, the money goes to their grandchildren, who get to receive it until they die. Boy, I really want a job.

Question: do you really think that if the government wanted to, they couldn't pay off the deficit, thus lowering the taxes of the citizens of the United States? I really don't think that there is a problem with the deficit. I think the situation the American people are facing is a result of good planning by the people we put into office, and I think they really like things the way they are. Spend, spend, spend, spend, spend.

Listen, they're spending our money frivolously like there's no tomorrow, and do you know why? That's simple: because neither you nor I can stop them. Did you notice what I said? I listed you and me as just two individuals working alone. What can anyone do by him or herself? Not much, but together, watch out, we can be a force to be reckoned with.

The petition here that needs signing is the one that our grandkids will be thanking us for, and that's the one that will pay off our deficit. We're going to do it any way we can.

Let's ask you a question: if money is tight, do you go out and spend like there's no tomorrow? Do you pay more for the item than it's worth, or do you shop around for the best price? You and I look for the best price; we don't go spend money that we don't have, but, as you know, our government does just that. They're wasting our money at an all-time high. *We need to stop them, and we need to stop them now.* If we do not stop them, all of us will be facing a future that will not be very bright. In fact, it's going to get so bad that all the bad will block out the sun which will kill us all.

Besides paying $85.00 for a pack of light bulbs and $37.50 for a box of paper clips, this is just one atrocity that they're doing with your money at a tune of $100,000 a year. Are you ready? Here we go—*next*. There is this woman in Iraq employed by one of those contractors hired by our government to rebuild that country.

What she does is she works in a tent where there are computers for the servicemen to use to check email or whatever, and when she sees that one of them gets up, she, for $100,000 a year, says, "Next."

It's funny to me that these men and women who we train how to run multi-million dollar machines can't for the life of them know for themselves when someone sitting at a computer is done and that if they are in the front of the line, they're next. That they need someone to tell them it's their turn boggles my mind.

Why is she there? Why do our employees spend our money that way? The answer is clear: it's because no one is telling them to stop, but if you sign this petition, they will.

That's what you get when you run a business without ever checking the books.

How come it is that the biggest employer, the U.S. government, only has one department that is self-supporting—the U.S. post office? For us to pay off this deficit, we're going to have to make other departments become self-supportive. In doing so, they will not need as much taxpayers' money to support any given department. Besides making some departments self-supportive, can there be other ways the government can help pay off the deficit? Let's allow big business to help.

If you were to put Coca-Cola on the U.S. postage stamp and charge them five hundred million dollars for six months, that would help to pay part of our deficit and even lower the cost of the stamp to twenty-five cents.

This petition, if signed, will allow big business to advertise on government property.

Can this happen if we all vote for them to do this for us? Listen, if we have to spend money, should we not spend the least amount possible? Should we open up an agency in our government that is kind of a watch dog for *We The People*, that kind of keeps an eye on them when they spend $85.00 for a light bulb and $37.50 for a box of paper clips, or should they just do their job? Again, there are those few simple words: *"just do their jobs."* Should we keep an eye on them, or should they do what we hired them for?

Okay, even with all the corruption that is going on in the government, look how good you and I have it now.

We really have it great, but I think that we can have it better!!! As one of their bosses, I say yes I want it better. What do you say?

When you drive down the freeway and you see the signs that tell you what street is coming up with how far you have to drive to get there, what's on the back side of them??? Nothing. So why don't we get the people that put the big billboards on the side of the road to put smaller ones on, charge big business for them, and use the money toward the deficit? Isn't it *We The People's* responsibility and not the government's?

Should *We The People* do the things that make it possible to pay off the deficit, or should you and I do nothing? J. Paul Getty said, "I would rather have one percent of a hundred men than one hundred percent of one," meaning that you can get more done when you do things together than by yourself. See, if we all vote on the things that we need to vote on and not the things that they tell us to vote on, then we will have a better life to live. Will you vote?

You know, I've been talking about responsibility of our government. What about the responsibility of *We The People*? And I don't just mean voting. I mean our responsibility for the opportunity for being able to live in a country for free—"free" is the key word. Should we live in this country for free, or should we pay? Well, we do pay for living in this country. We pay with our money in taxes and our blood, but I'm not talking about paying with money. I'm talking about paying with responsibility. So whose responsibility is it to pay off our deficit—our employees or ours? I think it's *We The People's* responsibility to tell our employees, the government, to find a way to pay off the deficit because if we don't pay it off, what do you think will happen? Well, I think that one of two things will happen.

1. Someone out there will pay it off, and we will be under their rule. You know, like, a bank gives you a loan and then sells your note to someone else, thus making you responsible to that person for paying off the note; or
2. We, the United States, declare bankruptcy and go to war, and then people die.

Well, I don't like either choice, so I think *We The People* should pay it off. Why us? Because *We The People* are the bosses, and it's our responsibility. So how do we do it? Well, I don't know, but I do know how to start. We raise money any way we can.

How about a lottery? We know that *We The People* love to gamble, and we also know that *We The People* spend a lot of money doing it.

The California lottery said, "If you let us do it, our schools will benefit from it." Well, guess what? They lied. So I think the government should take over all lotteries and use that money to pay off the deficit and not to go into the pockets of who knows. How about we generate money from foreign countries to help generate money? Maybe we should charge each person who visits our country $5.00 each time they visit.

How about each person living in our country pays $.01 each minute they talk on the phone? How much money would that generate?

Two-thirds of the population talks on the phone every day. How much money would that generate? Say we talk on the phone for ten minutes. That would be $.10 per person each day times 200,000,000 people, and that generates $2,000,000 each day. But what if we charged $.02? That would be $4,000,000 each day times 365 days a year equals $1,460,000,000 a year used toward paying off the deficit. All that money could be raised doing what we like doing, talking.

Can we afford not to do these things, or should we leave things alone and not care what the people that we put into office do? I mean, that's what we have been doing the past hundred years or so—allowing them to do whatever they want.

Do you like the way things are? Do you think things are going to get better if they keep doing the same things they have been doing in the past? I'm serious when I say this: *we need to end this way of governing and start fixing everything. We need a new government.*

If you really want to know the truth, our employees are not really doing what they want. They're doing what Corporate America wants because Corporate America gives our politicians money. In my world, that will not be tolerated anymore, and I'd like to send you, my employees, this message: "You better start doing your job and not what Corporate America says because I'll fire your ass if you don't begin. I believe that the other three hundred million bosses you have will tell you the same thing."

Now, I know no one likes spending money on some things, but paying off our deficit is **We The People's** responsibility, not our government's. Why? Because We The People are their bosses. And when is it the responsibility of employees to take care of keeping a business running? It's not. It's the bosses' job. We The People are the bosses, and we need to start acting like it.

We have freedom, and I believe we need to pay for it because of the saying "Anything worth anything can't be free."

What if we were to charge $.01 for each gallon of gas we purchase? It would be 10 to 20 gallons a week. That would be $.20 each week times 1/3 of the population = $1,400,000,000 each year at a cost of just $10.40 per person. Not bad at just $.20 each week. Can we afford that, or can we not afford to do it?

Can you think of other ways We The People can help pay off the deficit? I would sure like to hear from you, so please go to my web site at *www.towethepeople.com* and tell us your idea on how your idea will help all of us live a better life. If you know a problem that's out there, go to the web site and tell us of it, and we will find a solution to that problem using old-fashioned common sense.

How about getting rid of the cops giving us tickets for speeding or running red lights? How much money does it cost for a cop to stop us and give us a ticket? Well, there is their time for stopping us, the time at the station for paperwork, the time for the court to do their paperwork as well, etc. So how do we make it easier? We ticket ourselves.

We ticket ourselves with what is called a transponder. Some toll roads use them to bill customers who use the toll road instead of stopping to put in quarters. They just drive through an area where there is a device that reads the transponder on the dash of the car, and that person gets billed for what they use. So if we were to put a transponder in your car, then if you run a red light, the transponder goes off and in the mail you get billed for a ticket. Now the cost of the ticket no longer will cost you $100 plus because the computer kicks out the ticket and all they do is mail it to you at less cost because no cop is taking his time to give it to you. Also, by agreeing to have a transponder in your car, it shows the court that you are a good person. And for getting one, you get brownie points, or we just make them mandatory in all cars, thus forcing us to be better drivers.

Another thing that transponders would do is to help out police officers in high-speed chases. The transponder would have a device in it that would enable them to shut off the car, thus keeping the bad guy from crashing and maybe killing an innocent person. Also, it would keep the bad person from stealing the car in the first place knowing the transponder is there. A little cooperation with the authorities can make a big difference in the lives of many people.

How about using the military to help pay off the deficit? Want to fly in an F16 with a Navy pilot? $20,000 gets you a ride in one.

That money would pay the fuel costs or food for two hundred people. Pay costs for whatever, and they would start to become self-supportive. How about playing paintball war games with real soldiers? See how you compare with them. Or go on the rifle range at night to see a barrage of bullets with tracers bouncing off the hillside. Maybe even fire something. Hey, I know that if they said that I could drop a round and maybe even blow up something, I would be the first in line to give my money to do that kind of stuff.

How about going on an aircraft carrier and watching planes come and go? Maybe going on a battleship and aiming and firing one of their big guns, or maybe just getting to go on base to one of the officers' bars or lounges, meet *real heroes*, and hear war stories from veterans.

I think that the military can really generate a lot of money from the public, thus not needing as much of the tax dollars needed to support them. The deficit that we have now, which I will talk about later, is the way it is in part because of the amount of money that the military needs to keep doing what they've been doing. They are the biggest reason why we have a deficit now. So that is one of the biggest reasons why we need them to be self-supportive.

What other agencies or departments could be self-supportive? Are there certain agencies or departments that we could do without, causing the taxpayer to spend less?

There are many thing that we can come up with to help pay off the deficit and another one of my ideas is to let those people who drive on our freeways going near 200 MPH at three in the morning allowed to do it illegally by closing certain stretches of freeway between midnight and 6 in the morning on Sunday, have them pay $500.00 to go 20 miles up and 20 miles back at what ever pace they want if they and their car qualify safety standards we put into place. But wait there's more, on the other side of the freeway will be all the fans who will pay 10.00 to watch the cars go by as they sit on their cars safely behind the center divider.

We need a new system that will address all the things that We The People come up with that we want to do as long as we are responsible for our actions. What new idea do you want our government to let you do?

Chapter Six

Insurance and the Leech

This next petition will do two things. First, it will allow all of us to have the coverage needed to live a great life, and second, it will put murderers in jail.

How do you tell the difference between an insurance policy and a leech? The answer is you can't. They both suck. Literally. They suck you dry, leaving you with nothing. We spend hundreds of thousands of dollars for treatment that we're denied. *Why?*

Now, I'm not going to tell you of all the problems that are out there because you already know what they are. You've heard of them by watching TV or hearing from your friends. Still, all the same, I will tell you of just a few so as not to bore you.

This woman paid $36.50 each month for life insurance through her employer for years. She died, and when her family tried to get their money due them from them, they denied them their benefits.

This company, legally, did not have to pay these people their money that was due them, all because they didn't want to. Because they didn't want to? What kind of crap is that? Can you believe that crap? I mean, it smells like crap, sounds like crap, it must be crap. But it's no ordinary crap. This is special crap; in fact, it's corporate crap.

This company that she worked for uses third party administrators who are in charge of handling payments of life insurance. This company that she worked for is covered under the Employment Retirement Income Security Act. What that does for them is just what I stated; if they do not want to make good on any claim, then they and their third-party administrators are free from lawsuits under this act. Now let me ask you this: is your company you work for governed under this "thieving, taking-advantage-of-*We-The-People*, Corporate-America Crap Act"?

Let's take away the pieces of paper that take away from our ability to thrive.

Folks, when is enough enough? Is it enough when you're affected by it, or is it enough when your friends are affected, or is it when anyone is affected by it? There was this show on ABC called *Primetime: What Would You Do?* It was about what would you do in certain circumstances, and on one episode was a baby that was locked in a car by itself on a hot day. People would look in the car, see the baby crying, and then walk on by, leaving the baby in the car in over 120 percent of cases. Shame on all of you who didn't care about a possibly dying baby. I myself would have broken the window first and then called the police.

It matters to me when anyone suffers, and in this the greatest country in the world, there is a lot of suffering that doesn't have to happen.

Now, think about this one for a minute. A lot of the people that sell us insurance live in big houses, have fancy cars and pools, and live on golf courses. They really profit from our fear and sickness. Now, don't get me wrong. Some insurance policies are good and are needed. But the price we have to pay to have that security is too high, and it really should not be that way.

If *We The People* were to not give our money to insurance companies and all put our money into one pool, I believe that every person could have full coverage on everything from auto to health. There are over three hundred million people in the United States, and if we were to pay $10.00 each month, we would have in excess of over three billion each month to pay for the people's need for coverage.

If we were to charge you every month regardless of how much money is in the kitty, then at the end of the year all the money that has not been used up because of medical purposes and the like goes to pay off the deficit. If ten dollars a month is not enough money, then we'll make it $20, giving us $6 billion for the coverage.

Six billion dollars—that's huge A Month.

Wouldn't that be great, if all that money were to go to the doctors and the hospitals and there were no insurance companies taking their part?

Insurance companies are in business to make money, not make sure that you who pay them that money receive the best treatment and medicines. Let's do away with all those blood-sucking leeches.

Do you know what a leech is? It's a thing that attaches itself to your body and takes and takes and takes and never gives anything back. When they, the leeches, discover that you need something done to help cure yourself, a horrible thing happens. They find a loophole where they, the bloodsuckers, don't have to give you the treatment you paid for.

Did you know that when not the doctors or their administration but the insurance companies deny you coverage that you're entitled to and you die from a lack of treatment, that's called murder? And do you also know that the government knows that those murders take place, and they do nothing? It's wrong, and it needs to change *now*.

If you haven't figured it out by now, our government does not want us to have socialized medicine all because they and their Corporate American friends will loose billions of dollars. Certain people in the government will lose billions in kickbacks and the insurance people will lose billions also, and so I say, *so be it*

Do you see what I am trying to do here? I'm trying to make you aware that there are indeed things that we can do together to make our lives better.

If the government doesn't want to help us do this, then this is just another thing that we can do together without their help. We'll just have a 900 number to call and leave your name, etc. You will be registered for the month, and if something happens to you, we'll take care of it.

For every phone call that comes into the phone company, they will bill the customer, taking out their fee and sending the rest to a fund that bears interest to be used as necessary. Kind of exciting, don't you think? Don't you think that we should do whatever it takes to make a better life for all of us? If we need health insurance, should we not all have it? Does it only belong to those who can afford it? Does someone have to die because they don't have five dollars for health insurance? Is three to six billion dollars a month enough for health coverage for everybody?

When you give your money to an insurance company, they take your money and give it to their employees. They pay building costs and utilities. They pay whatever it takes to run the business and make a profit, kind of just like any other business out there, with one exception. For their hard work, the owners of these companies receive the pleasure of making sure all their customers are satisfied and remain happy. Remember the saying "The customer is always right"? Well, that does not apply to these companies. They're in it for themselves and do not give a rat's ass for their customers. They prove it daily by denying treatment so they won't lose money. They profit, and we die.

There are, in our country right now, over fifty million people who do not have health coverage, and eighteen thousand of them will die this very year as a result of that.

There's a man out there (and I'm sure there are many who are in the same boat he's in) who is seventy-nine years old who is forced to keep working, all because Medicare doesn't cover the cost of the medicine that he and his wife need.

This woman got into a car crash and was unconscious, and she was not able to call her insurance company first before being transported to the hospital. As a result of being unconscious and unable to call them, she got stuck with the bill for the ambulance ride.

This one woman was approved for all medical treatment totaling over $7,000.00. Then the insurance company discovered that in the past she had a yeast infection. She lost her health coverage all because she did not disclose that information before signing her application. The insurance took back the money they paid to the doctors and told them that if they wanted to get paid they would have to get it from her themselves.

Do I have to go on telling you the things that these insurance companies do? I'm sure you know many things that they have done as well.

If you want to stop these blanked-de-blank-blank companies and want our employees to do their jobs and protect us from all blood sucking leeches, whoever they may be, then make a difference and *vote*.

I don't know if any of you are religious or not, but did you know that the one dollar bill is a god? It has the power to give or take life, and the people who worship that god have millions of them.

> The CEO of Humana, Mike McCallister, made 3.3 million gods in just one year.
>
> John Rowe, CEO of Aetna, made 22.2 million gods in just one year.
>
> Bill McGuire, CEO of UnitedHealth, made a whopping 1.6 *billion* gods, and all of them don't care if you live or die.

Question: why do you give them your money? Why don't we just cut them out of the equation and go to the source? Why do we need a middle man? And it's not just one middle man, it's thousands of them getting your money, and what's left over is given to the health professionals to take care of you if the middle man says it's okay. We have to ask them first if it's okay if we get healthy with the money we gave them to do just that.

This can be a reality if everyone calls. If you don't call, no one will benefit. If you haven't yet discovered it, this book is all about what we can do together as a nation if we want to. If we decide to do this, then we can truly say with honor that, for the first time in the existence of the United States, we are now truly united, a true United States. I think that would be wonderful.

Socialized medicine, *they* say, is a bad thing. Wait a minute, who are *they*? Um, could it be the tooth fairy? No, probably not. How about Santa Claus? No, not him either. Oh, I know, it's those religious ones who the all-powerful god influences, the ones who worship the one dollar bill.

Do you like your fire department? Socialized, how about your public library? Socialized, schools? Socialized, police department, socialized as well, and they think we can't socialize the health care in our country because it won't work, I bet if you were to take money out of the equation that we would be there now.

People come up with bills and hope they will become laws to better all of society, and they get shot down. Could it be because it conflicts with the shooter's own hidden agendas?

If you want to see how a medical plan for everyone would work go to

http://www.pnhp.org/facts/singlepayer_fa . . .

Chapter Seven

Consumer Reports

Consumer Reports is a magazine that rates all of the products. It is easy to understand, which, in my opinion, is a great way to understand all the issues and maybe even a great way to, for the first time, really know whom we are voting for. Put the candidates on a graph to show where they will stand on all issues. Find out who is the best qualified for the job so we can vote. Hey, I want the best working for me. Just like when you hire an employee to work for you; you want the best of all the applicants who applied for that job. Don't you? Well, I want that kind of simple-to-understand information so I can vote for the best person for the job. The information that they give us nowadays is sometimes difficult to understand, thus not making it easy to vote.

This is not just my own opinion but that of others as well. President George Bush Sr. was the most qualified president this country has ever seen. He had accomplished the most of any other president that we have ever had according to the qualifications for the job. I never knew about his qualifications because no one told me about them. And I would not know where to go to start looking. But if it were on a graph like *Consumer Reports* does, it would be very simple for me to make an educated decision based upon that type of information. The next petition that needs signing is making sure that, if you live in our country and are a citizen, it is mandatory that you vote if you are of legal age because how can a company run itself when the bosses don't tell the employees what to do?

I think that in these days that we live, just about every person we have in government signed up with ulterior motives. Hey, again, it's not their fault that the government is the way it is now. The blame goes to the ones in this country who quit or stopped voting. But that's not true either because the blame, in my opinion, rests solely on the shoulders of the person in the government who made voting a difficult thing.

I'm going to use Arnold Schwarzenegger as an example. There was this TV commercial saying that he took money from a school fund to be used for something else and he never repaid the loan he took from that fund. And then there's this other commercial that comes on that says not only did he not take the money from that school fund but says that he even gave a large amount of money to the school. *Who's lying*, and, more importantly, why does the government allow these lies to go on TV and confuse us on how we should vote? How are we supposed to run this country of ours when our employees won't tell us the truth about all the issues? See, they don't want us to know the real truth. And I wonder why. Could greed be a possible answer?

A long time ago we quit voting. And they took over, and we never saw it coming. I'm to blame as well. A lot of the time, I didn't vote. Sometimes I have voted for half of the things on the ballot and am just as guilty as the rest of you who do the same. My excuse is that on certain issues the people who make up the information they give us so we can investigate the issues and make our decision accordingly have made them so damn difficult to understand that we just say, "yeah, right" and don't vote. Ulterior motives? You bet.

The government we have now, I believe, wants to keep us all ignorant and not let us know what's going on because if we knew what they really did, they know that they would not have a job anymore. So they give us the information they want us to have and not the truth, thus keeping us blind to the truth.

If *We The People* really knew whom we were voting for, they probably would have not won. It would probably have been the person who ran for office that you knew nothing about. The little guy running only gets a few thousand votes, and they were probably the best qualified. And we, as a people, only knew what they wanted us to know.

Those little guys had no money to run for office, so the public knew not of them. I think that we should make campaigning the same for everyone who runs. Give the little guys the same opportunities that the big boys have. Put them all on graphs. Give them all fifteen minutes to tell us why they should be hired for the job. Make it simple and make it fair so we can get the best.

Make all contributions be equally divided among all candidates to give everyone the same opportunity.

Chapter Eight

Article II, Section 4

This petition is my favorite of them all that need signing.

Article II, Section 4 of the Constitution states "that the president, vice president and all civil officers of the United States, shall be removed from office on impeachment for, and conviction of, treason, bribery or other high crimes"!! Is it true? Is it true that they in the government have that power to impeach any or all people in office who break those laws, or is it true that *We The People* have that power to impeach them? If it is *We The People*, then how do we find out who did wrong so we can kick them out? Can we truly find out? I bet the people in government would say that it is almost impossible to find out and then convict them.

Remember the part that said impeachment for treason, bribery, or other high crimes? Well, I don't know what high crimes are, but I do know what bribery is. I believe that in every department in the government, crime is present. Remember, this government is run by greed, so this crime has to happen all the time, right? I bet it is everywhere, and just about everyone is doing it, from building inspectors to judges to lawyers to government contracting, *etc, etc, etc.*

I don't think that it is an assumption on my part but a fact. It is present in our everyday lives. We see it all the time. I myself, in construction, see it with city inspectors.

City inspectors come in to make sure that in every aspect of construction all laws will be adhered to. Well, not all the time. Is bribery present? Here are two true examples.

1. There were townhomes that were built near a creek, and when the earthquake of Northridge, California, happened, quite a few of the units jumped right off the foundation. Why? Because someone who was in charge of bolting down the units didn't do his job. So it's his fault. All he had to do was look to see if the nuts and washers were securely fastened to the bolts that come out of the concrete. It was just that easy.

When they opened up all the walls of the units
that jumped off their foundations, they found that all
the washers and nuts were lying on the side next to
the bolts. No one, I guess, took the time to make
sure the units were bolted down.

Yes, I want them building my house. I'll supply the beer.

2. This example is of a city inspector who was employed by a school. The fire sprinkler installer had to be somewhere in hurry one day, I guess, so he just glued the sprinkler heads to the ceiling tiles. There were no pipes connected, just the heads glued on the ceiling. So whose fault was this, the plumber or the inspector? I wonder? Hey, this is not a house jumping off its foundation; it is the possible death of your kids and friends. To me, this is a biggie. My question is, did that inspector get fired or impeached? I don't know. Do you?

Those were just two examples where bribery could be present.

When the Northridge quake happened, a lot of bad things happened. People died. Did some of them die because the city inspectors didn't do their jobs? Did all or any of them get fired? Did our government go after the contractors who did the work? Are they in jail for murder? Are the city inspectors in jail for those crimes as well?

Hey, people died in the Northridge quake because someone who *We The People* put into office did not do their job. Was bribery possible in any of the cases that came up? Was bribery possible in any of the deaths in the Northridge quake? I still don't know what high crimes are, but I do know what treason is.

Treason is an act or an instance of disloyalty to deceive by trust and the betrayal of trust. Do you think that treason can be present with bribery in some cases? As big as the government is, I believe that treason happens all the time.

Did you know that in wartime treason is punishable by death?

What's my point here? If all this crime exists and nothing happens, then it has to be because the government, again, likes it that way. Keep doing things in secret and keeping the people ignorant. Can we as a people really find out and end the games that our employees are playing? I think we can. We vote. We go back and investigate the people that were responsible for paying $85.00 for one light bulb and $37.50 for a paper clip, and we start with them. How about it?

Did you know that I left out something in Article II, Section 4 of the Constitution?

We The People can impeach the president, vice president, and all civil officers on misdemeanor charges. Do you think our employees are committing misdemeanors and getting away with them? Well, I do. Just a little while ago, a judge was convicted of drunk driving for the eighth time, and all that happened to him on his eighth charge was a $100.00 fine.

Should this judge and all other judges be exempt from the laws that apply *To We The People*?

I am not saying I want to fire anyone from the government. *I just want them to do their jobs.* If they don't want to do their jobs and they won't quit, then we fire them.

I can just imagine the conversation our forefathers must have had when they wrote this article. I like to think it went something like this:

"Okay, how do we fire one of us from the position that we now hold?" "Why do we need something like that? Aren't we all going to do our jobs to the best of our ability?" "Yes, but when we're all gone and our country is run by other people, they might not want to do their jobs fully. And they might have other ideas that will inherently come with having these jobs." "Whatever do you mean George?" "Well, let's assume that someone out there contacts you and offers you a bribe to pass a bill or make a new law that will benefit them over someone else or a corporation. We need a way to fire them because they committed treason." "Wait, who said anything about treason?" "Oh come on, how is it that you're one of the leaders of this country, and you don't know what treason is?" "When you fail at keeping your oath to do your job properly and have other ulterior motives, that's treason." "Thanks, George." "Don't thank me, thank God we're honest. That sort of thing won't apply to us." "Yes, but what other things besides treason should be a way to impeach someone for failing to uphold their oath?"

"I know. We must include bribery as well." "Good one, John, what else?"

"How about-" "Oh, I know, how about making high crimes a way to impeach someone?" "Yes, good. What else should be a way?" "How about, um-" "Now remember guys, this is only going to apply to those like us, the leaders of-" "Wait a minute. It should not only apply to the president and vice president but to all civil officers as well." "Wow, Joey, you finally came up with a good idea on your own, 'atta boy." "I told you, George, to quit calling me 'Joey'." "Ok, just kidding. Anyway, so what we have so far is bribery, treason, and high crimes. I think that should do it. What do you all say?" "Yup, we all concur."

Finishing up cleaning the dishes from the dinner table where this conversation took place that mid-summer's eve back some two hundred years ago was this fine, young-looking, strapping young man who must have looked like me. No, not you, the reader who is reading this, but I, myself, the writer of these fine words. Anyway, this young man said, with dishes in hand, to all that were there that evening so long ago, "Why don't you make it so that if any of you commit as low as a misdemeanor you can get impeached?" As I walked to the kitchen with both hands full of dish—wait a minute, as that strapping young man was walking, he heard someone in the room say, "Why should we allow such a minimal offense be a way to get impeached?"

Without missing a beat, the boy said, "Because you people have been appointed to this office of honor by God. You have the greatest job in the world. You get to serve others. All these people that voted for you to do your job of running this country for them trust you and believe that you'll do what you say you'll do. You should be above reproach. All of you are role models to a lot of people out there. You have a life that most people want. You don't have the luxury to falter in any way with such a huge responsibility set before you. Yes, any one of you who takes advantage of your position should lose your job that easily."

I got an e-mail from one of my friends informing that as of right now, that of the 535 members of Congress, over 450 are now eligible for impeachment?

I say we start the impeachment process on all of them who put themselves before *we the people.*

Chapter Nine

Judges

Well, now that you got me talking about judges, I believe that they should, to some degree, be held accountable for their actions. They are now exempt from recourse. Here are two examples:

1. This one judge had a case before him regarding this seven-to-ten-year-old girl who had a venereal disease. Do you know how you contract VD? You can only get it from one source—having sex. The judge said that there was no proof that the person who was watching her, who also had VD, sexually abused her and that sex was not necessarily the only way to get it, so he let the guy go.
2. These people went fishing and caught a shark. When they gutted the shark, they found a man's forearm with a rose tattoo. The police put a picture of the tattoo on the news, and this girl called up and said that it was her husband or boyfriend's arm. There was an investigation. It was found that the man's friends all went deep sea fishing, and they killed him and stuffed him into a big trunk. But they couldn't get his arm into the trunk, so they tied the trunk shut with rope, left his arm hanging out, and threw him overboard. Well, a shark came swimming by and had a quick snack. The men confessed to murdering the man. The judge let them go because he said that there was no proof and that there could be a man walking around society somewhere with no arm.

I'm sure you have been privy to other things that you have heard about where someone in the service to the people did not do their job properly. Come on folks, *We The People* have to start to take our responsibilities seriously. We are their bosses, and we have to tell them what to do. How many of you out there let your employees do whatever they want? You're the boss, and you tell them what to do. They do it, and if they don't do what you say, they don't work for you anymore. So why is this any different? They're our employees, aren't they?

So how do we fire them??? Well one guy in our government thinks like I do and he is **State Rep. Charlie Brown and he wants a plan allowing public to recall local officials he said** "I believe the people of Indiana deserve the right to remove their duly elected officials whenever they act in a manner that violates the trust placed in them," he continued. "There are too many examples to mention here that demonstrate the need for a recall process to be put in place, but they all emphasize the need for a continual check against any abuses committed against the public."

> Under Brown's proposal, a person can begin the recall process by obtaining a petition from the county clerk's office, then obtaining the signatures of at least 10 percent of the registered voters in the district or political subdivision of the official who is subject to the recall.

> "An official can be removed if a majority of the registered voters in the specified election district vote for the recall," Brown said.

Well, if we can't impeach them because of something they didn't do wrong, then when it comes time to vote to keep them in their position, we vote for someone else.

But we have got to vote. Please vote.

Again, I'm not trying to down the United States, but there are things that we have wrong with our government; they are all fixable. I believe if we just keep trying to make it better, it will happen. Did you see the key word here is *try*? If we tried, good things would happen. It seems the government that we have now doesn't want to try to make things better. The proof is that when crimes are committed, they do nothing about them. Why is that? I'm serious. But it's all going to change because you are going to vote, aren't you?

When I do construction work for a customer, I am held accountable for my actions. So are you. So why should not our employees be? This petition will make all of our judges think before just spitting out sentences as haphazardly as they can do now.

Chapter Ten

Heroes

There is something else wrong with this government we have, and it's how they treat my heroes, the men and women who put their lives on the line for all of us to have the security of no harm coming to us from any domestic or foreign power. Those people who fought in wartime are my heroes. Those people who put their life on the line every day in our cities, policemen and firemen, they are my heroes. I believe that we should take care of them. They are the reason we have the life we have, and I just want to say thank you to all of you who put your lives on the line for me and my family and friends.

I hate seeing vets who are homeless and who our government just seems to turn its back on and not care. Well, shame on you.

My brother is a vet, not from wartime but peacetime. Anyway, he was sitting in the VA hospital, and this other vet sitting next to him died while waiting for his turn. Going to the VA, I understand, is an all-day event. Does it have to be?

The Gulf War, I believe, as do other people, was a chemical war. It was reported that Saddam Hussein was using chemical weapons on our troops the first time Bush Sr. sent our troops over there. According to the doctors for the government, there is no proof that the men and women who put their lives on the line for us were exposed to any kind or form of said weapons. Yeah, just like Agent Orange didn't exist. We need to start taking care of our servicemen who get sick and not turn our backs on them. I'll say it again: they are the reason that we have our freedom, so maybe we should reward those who spend time fighting for our country. Haven't they earned it? I think that if we all vote to better society, there will be money in surplus and we can start to take care of them better. Don't they deserve it? Should we not treat them better?

Back at home, the families of a lot of the servicemen that are fighting for us are on food stamps because they make very little money keeping our country safe. That's just another thing that's wrong.

REMEMBER THE HEROES OF 911????? when they got sick from inhaling all the stuff in the air as the result of the Twin Towers coming down our wonderful government those absolute fantastic people who We The People put into office turned their back on them and said in a loud voice "Go SCREW yourselves, we're not going to help you get healthy even though you put your life on the line for our dying police and firefighters that day so long ago, you're not worth anything to us so again in a loud voice GO SCREW YOURSELVES"

These petitions need signing for all of our heroes.

Here's one of my thoughts. If I were the president, when it came up about kicking Saddam Hussein out of Kuwait, I would have told him if he didn't get out of there and he forced us to go over there to kick him out, I would send him a bill for the war. We would add up every penny spent, from paper clips to water, and he would be responsible *To We The People* for it. For every U.S. serviceman that was to die, he would have to pay $100,000 to the family for their loss. Injure any one of them, and you will have to pay them $100,000 to $1,000,000 for their injury. Forewarned is fair warned.

The first petition that needs to be signed is that all servicemen or servicewomen who go into battle and are in the shit—and not five hundred miles behind enemy lines but the ones who see all the horrors of war—will, for their sacrifice, never have to pay income taxes again unless they make over $55,000 or more a year.

The second petition that we need to sign is that all servicemen or servicewomen who get injured in battle can go to any hospital and see any doctor they want. And the last petition that we need to sign is described in the "Iraq War for Sale" chapter.

Chapter Eleven

Crime and the Prison System

In this day and age which we live, in this greatest country in the world, we have another problem, which is crime.

It's scary nowadays how crime has become the norm. It seems that you can't trust anyone anymore. If you think about it, we allow the criminals to dictate how we live. They set the rules by which we live. Also, they make us do things that we would not normally do, like walk across the street to avoid them and look in the back seat of our cars before we get in just to see if someone is hiding there.

Crime, as it is now in our country, is only going to get worse. The more the population grows, the more our government doesn't enforce laws. What? What did I say? Laws are not being enforced. Well, it's true, and we'll go into that later.

Criminals are getting much bolder than ever before, and it's only going to get worse unless *We The Good People* of the United States put our foot down and say enough is enough. I am sure there are far more good people in the United States than there are bad. If we all come together, we can just about nip crime in the bud. If you want to be a criminal, you're just going to have to go do it somewhere else. If the criminals in this country want to keep on being bad, then we'll put you in a place where you can be as bad as you want because *We The Good People* won't care what you do because you won't be around anymore to bother us.

Did you see the movie *Escape from New York*? To sum it up, they had one rule: once you go in, you never come out. We need to come up with a place where we can do something like this. Give the prisoners a way to be self-supportive, and they can be there forever, never to bother us again. Let's take San Clemente Island in California and turn it into a prison. Let's give the criminals the resources to be self supporting and have only one rule: once you go in, you never come out. Go into the desert somewhere, and create a city that people can live there and not in our own cities. Welcome to your new life. There's your food. There's your shelter. See ya.

I believe that if we implement this kind of system, it will be a real deterrent and you will see a real reduction in crime.

I believe the criminals who have a long track record behind them have proven to the world that they just don't care about you or me, and so they will continue to take the rights of their victims away by committing crimes against them.

Well, since they just don't care about us, let's get rid of them. Tell all criminals who have a track record that if they get picked up one more time, they are gone. Make it known what their fate will be after a certain number of offenses.

There are two types of criminals out there, good ones and bad ones, so there should be two types of jails and two sets of rules.

There are some good people who do make mistakes, so they should not be put in jail with the real hardened criminals.

One of the biggest reasons we should not put good people in with bad people is that when we do, those people come out of prison bad people.

Just about all the inmates who were polled said that they never did hard drugs until they went to prison. Also, they said that they now know how to commit crimes they never thought of doing and how easy it is to do them and get away with them. This includes murder.

The majority of people in prison or county jail are there because of drug-related crimes. Good people having bad luck with being hooked on drugs do crimes to get their drugs. I think that all people who get busted for doing drugs should get house arrest and leave the jails open only to really bad people. No longer should we live our lives by the rules the criminals make for us. I refuse to live my life by their rules any more.

Look people, there are more good people in this country than bad; we can, if we all come together, stomp out crime in our communities. We will just not tolerate it anymore. We need to tell them that *forewarned is fair warned*. If you want to be bad, that's fine, just go to another country and have a party, but don't do it in my backyard.

It can be that simple if we all decide that we want a life free of fear and crime. Look, the bad people are only bad because they choose to be. Well, if they have that kind of freedom to be bad and possibly harm others and myself, well, then I should have the right to not want the bad people living around me.

Do you know what the first thing that happens to all victims of crime is? They all have this in common: they all had their *rights* taken away from them by the criminal. So I think that the first thing that should be taken from them, the criminal, is *all their rights*, all of them, not just some of them but all of them. And turn them into the property of the U.S. government.

Now, you're going to talk about the *criminal's* rights, but I say to you, "Shut up." They took away the rights of the victim, so they lose all rights. Do you know what kind of games criminals nowadays can play because they have rights?

Example: This one guy in prison right now has four cells to his name, all filled with court stuff, and he ties up the courts every year with frivolous lawsuits. He is costing the taxpayers millions. What's wrong with this picture? He has rights. Why? I believe that his rights should not be his rights anymore.

The reason I say that we need two sets of rules is because sometimes good people do stupid things, and when they go to court, they get hammered by the courts. Maybe they get hammered because the judges have hardened hearts because of all the bad people that have come before them, and they can't distinguish the good from the bad.

If you sign this petition, then all of our grandchildren will grow up not knowing the horrors we have before us now.

Chapter Twelve

Aggregate, the Hammer, And the Illegal

A long time ago, there was a man who owned this aggregate rock quarry where he employed men to break up the rocks that couldn't be lifted by one man into a cart. That was their job. It was a backbreaking job, and most people didn't want to do it because of that reason. Well, the owner got more orders for his aggregate but could not fill them because he had not enough people to break up the rocks. He was losing money, so he went to the government to ask for their help. He wanted to use prisoners to break up the rocks and, in return, pay the government for the use of the prisoners' labor. Hence, the term *hard labor* was invented.

What a great idea. Use convicts to do the work that Americans didn't want to do. Think about it. What if we did that same thing today? Would the cost of lettuce be lower if we got them to do the picking? What would happen to the people doing that job now? Well, I guess we would deport them back to wherever they came from, *right*? I mean, aren't the ones who pick the food that we eat here living illegally?

I know that, since I am an American, if you were to hire me to do that hard labor, the stores would have to charge you ten dollars for that lettuce because the cost of labor to pick it was too expensive. So maybe that's why they do the picking and not me, and maybe that's why our government, which knows that they are there doing the picking, does nothing about it. They do nothing because the cost would be too much, and, all around would be bad for the economy.

Do you think that, if they wanted to, they could round up all the illegal aliens and deport them? The answer is yes, they could, but they don't. *How come?* Because we as Americans need to have cheap labor in order to fill our bellies at a reasonable cost. It's good for the economy to have cheap labor.

How much do the farmers pay the illegals each hour to work? Three dollars or five dollars an hour? Let's do the math. You have twenty workers in the field at $5.00 each hour. That's $100.00 an hour that the farmer has to pay to get his food to the market. Let's just say they work ten hours a day and five days a week, and they need at least four weeks to bring in the crop. How much did the farmer have to pay? $20,000.00. But what if he were to only have to pay $4,000.00 for the same laborers? He would make more money, and so he could sell to the stores for less because he would have made up the difference in cost-saving labor. The stores would then be able to sell the produce to the consumer for less, saving us money, and everybody would win, even the laborers who do the work for only $10.00 per day would be happy doing it.

I met a man who worked in a prison as a correction officer who was in charge of picking inmates who would get to work in the prison for $0.50 a day. Somehow this correction officer got permission to hire these inmates to work outside the prison and pay them $1.00 per day as opposed to their normal rate of $0.50, and the inmates lined up to get the privilege to get to work outside of the prison and make double the pay.

If we were to hire them to do the picking, then everybody would win, and the farmers would not have to hire illegals to do their work. Maybe if we do this, then our government will not allow them to live here anymore. Just a little while ago, a lot of illegals came together and, on the same day, did not show up for work. When asked why, they said they wanted to show Americans that we needed them here to do the work that Americans didn't want to do. Boy, they showed us, didn't they?

But do you understand what they really said? They said that they were going to show *Americans*. Americans made this country by spilling their blood for us a long time ago and today. Americans give their money so that our employees can run this country of ours then and now. Two questions: what do all the illegal aliens who are here in our country have in common? And why do they want to come to the land of the free? And the answer to the second question is just that, it's free to them. It doesn't cost them anything, and if they choose to be bad, most of the time they don't go to jail. We deport them, and then they walk over the border just to do the same thing again. And our government allows this, all because they want cheap labor.

The answer to the first question is that they all want to come here because we are free in this great country of ours to do and be anything that we want to be. They just want all that we have to offer for free and to not have to pay. And just in case you weren't privy to this, we *Americans* are paying for them to live here for *free*. Some of the people who get into our country do not want to be bad and do want to be apart of our country but they must do it legally and since we know that they want to be here then maybe we should help them out by not making it so hard for them to get here, but a lot of them just want it for free and don't want to pay with their money or with their blood. So since they don't want to become *real Americans,* I think that we need to tell our government that we want them deported back to wherever they came from and asked politely to not come back. Then we need to *mine the borders* so no one can come over here illegally anymore.

If we mine our borders how many people do you think will die the first year doing so? 5 maybe 10 because after that they will get the message and not try that way anymore because they will know that they will die. On average more than 4,000 illegal aliens die in our deserts each year due to getting lost at night and in a few days die from lack of water, so mining our borders will in effect save lives. Listen; our government wants the illegals here, and the proof is that they are here.

If this doesn't make you stop and think, nothing will.

At a tune of $338.3 billion each and every year, illegal aliens cost this much money to the taxpayers of our country, and you can check it out for yourself. Please do so.

1. $11 billion to $22 billion is spent on welfare to illegal aliens each year (*http://tinyurl.com/zob77*).
2. $2.2 billion a year is spent on food assistance programs such as food stamps, WIC, and free school lunches for illegal aliens (*http://www.cis.org/articles/2004/fiscalexec.html*).
3. $2.5 billion a year is spent on Medicaid for illegal aliens (*http://www.cis.org/articles/2004/fiscalexec.html*).
4. $12 billion a year is spent on primary and secondary school education for children here illegally, and they cannot speak a word of English! (*http://transcripts.cnn.com/TRANSCRIPTS/0604/01/ldt.0.html*)
5. $17 billion a year is spent for education for the American-born children of illegal aliens, known as anchor babies (*http://transcripts.cnn.com/TRANSCRIPTS/0604/01/ldt.01.html*).
6. $3 million a *day* is spent to incarcerate illegal aliens (*http://transcripts.cnn.com/TRANSCRIPTS/0604/01/ldt.01.html*).
7. 30 percent of all federal prison inmates are illegal aliens (*http://transcripts.cnn.com/TRANSCRIPTS/0604/01/ldt.01.html*).
8. $90 billion a year is spent on illegal aliens for welfare and social services by the American taxpayers (*http://premium.cnn.com/TRANSCIPTS/0610/29/ldt.01.html*).
9. $200 billion a year in suppressed American wages are caused by the illegal aliens (*http://transcripts.cnn.com/TRANSCRIPTS/0604/01/ldt.01.html*).
10. The illegal aliens in the United States have a crime rate that's two and a half times that of white, non-illegal aliens. In particular, their children are going to make a huge additional crime problem in the United States (*http://transcripts.cnn.com/TRANSCRIPTS/0606/12/ldt.01.html*).

11. During the year of 2005 there were four to ten *million* illegal aliens that crossed our southern border. Also, as many as nineteen thousand and five hundred illegal aliens from terrorist countries crossed our borders. Millions of pounds of drugs, cocaine, meth, heroin, and marijuana crossed into the United States from the southern border (Homeland Security Report: *http://tinyurl.com/t9sht*).
12. The National Policy Institute "estimated that the total cost of mass deportation would be between $206 and $230 billion or an average cost of between $41 and $46 billion annually over a five year period" (*http://www.nationalpolicyinstitute.org/pdf/deportation.pdf*).
13. In 2006, illegal aliens sent home $45 *billion* in remittances back to their countries of origin (*http://www.rense.com/general75/niht.htm*).
14. "The Dark Side of Illegal Immigration: Nearly One Million Sex Crimes Committed by Illegal Immigrants In The United States."

So let's secure our borders and give that money
to our people so we can thrive.
These statistics are from California alone:

1. 40 percent of all workers in L. A. County (L. A. County has 10.2 million people) are working for cash and not paying taxes. This is because they are predominantly illegal immigrants working without a green card.
2. 95 percent of warrants for murder in Los Angeles are for illegal aliens.
3. 75 percent of people on the most-wanted list in Los Angeles are illegal aliens.
4. Over 2/3 of all births in Los Angeles County are to illegal alien Mexicans on Medi-Cal whose births were paid for by taxpayers.
5. Nearly 35 percent of all inmates in California detention centers are Mexican nationals here illegally.
6. Over three hundred thousand illegal aliens in Los Angeles County are living in garages.
7. The FBI reports half of all gang members in Los Angeles are most likely illegal aliens from south of the border.
8. Nearly 60 percent of all occupants of HUD properties are illegal.
9. Twenty-one radio stations in L. A. are Spanish speaking.
10. In L. A. County, 5.1 million people speak English and 3.9 million speak Spanish.(There are 10.2 million people in L. A. County.)

(All ten of the above are from the Los Angeles Times)

Less than 2 percent of illegal aliens are picking our crops, but 29 percent are on welfare. Over 70 percent of the United States's annual population growth (and over 90 percent of annual population growth in California, Florida, and New York) results from immigration. Approximately 29 percent of inmates in federal prisons are illegal aliens.

Don't you think that if our government really didn't want them here, they wouldn't be here anymore? Well, I propose that we tell our government that we want convicts to do the work that illegals do so we can clean up our country and keep all illegals out. This will be great for all of us.

Some of you might think that I am prejudiced against certain people. Well you're damn right, I don't like anyone who is bad and wants to do harm to the innocent, regardless of what country they might come from.

Chapter Thirteen

Brownie Points, Lawyers, and The Insurance Companies

Ever wonder why it seems that just about everyone just doesn't care about anyone anymore? Ever wonder why? Well, this petition will change that forever. I think it's because we feel that it doesn't pay to help people out anymore because you never know.

This one guy that I read about stopped to help this person out on the freeway, and the person pulled out a shotgun, killed the good bystander, and then stole his car. That is why bad people stop me from helping others out. I'm afraid now, so why should I bother? I don't ride a motorcycle anymore for the same reason, and that's because I have a responsibility to my family to keep myself alive.

I think we need to set up a system where good people who help others get brownie points to show the courts who is good and who is bad so we can be dealt with differently. Okay, how do we give brownie points to people?

Get brownie points for stopping at an accident and being a witness as to what really happened. I'm sure that there are many things that we can do to get BP if we want to. Now, what if some people were to take in a homeless person? What benefit would there be for that person to do it? *Brownie points?*

How about *We The People* get brownie points for being respectful toward the police officer when *We The People* do wrong? *We The People* are the ones doing wrong, and they are only doing their job. For us to take out our anger on them is wrong. Maybe a way to show the cops who the good people are is to start a new program called *Adopt a Cop*.

Yeah, find a police officer, sheriff, or HWP, and take them to lunch or have them over for dinner to show our support. Remember, they're people too.

Why do parents give their children money as an allowance each week? So their child cleans up his or her room—kind of like bribery, right? If you do something that I want you to do, I will give you something you want.

Well, what if our government were to do that as well? What do you think would happen?

How about giving blood to the Red Cross? Would doing so end the shortage of blood they need? Would that also end the commercials that the Red Cross has to do at a great cost to them? So take that money they spend, and put it to a greater cause, like doing what they do best—helping people who need help. Get brownie points for giving blood. If that were so, would more people give blood?

If five to twelve people stop at any given accident to document what happened, then the information gathered by the police from the five plus witnesses gets to the judge, and based on the witnesses' testimony, the judge renders the person at fault right away instead of having to go to court and waste the taxpayers' money. Being that all these witnesses come forward to testify as to what really happened, the person who is at fault would know that indeed they were wrong and must admit to being wrong so as to not have to go to court. The people who come forward to tell the truth get points, and the person who admits that the witnesses are telling the truth also gets points for telling the truth and saving the taxpayers' money.

If the person who is at fault says that all the witness are lying and/or are mistaken, wants to go to court to try to get off of the charges, and is found guilty, his punishment will be tripled due to lying. Kind of a deterrent, don't you think? Remember, I do not have all the answers, but I have a lot of ideas as to how we could cut through the red tape and get to the bottom line so we can move forward with our lives.

As soon as a judge renders a person guilty and as soon as the person who was not at fault goes through rehab and therapy, the cost that the person gets from the insurance company is three times the doctor's bill; 45 percent will go to the person insured, 30 percent to the doctors, and 25 percent to the lawyers.

No more two-years-plus to go to court to come up with that very decision, that you get three times the doctor's bill. Let's just cut to the chase. When we have a lot of witnesses to come forward as to what really happened, it will work.

Did you like how I split up the money from the insurance company for the accident? Well, it gets better.

The person injured gets 70 percent, the doctors get 30 percent, and the lawyers get 0 percent because if five or more witnesses come forward and testify what they saw, we just make it so that even a cop can just forward, via the computer, that Joe Blow is indeed guilty according to the witnesses. Thus, we will not need to go to court and waste the tax dollars to come up with the same decision. Or, allow the police officer to have the ability to be a judge as well so he can render a decision right there, and he will be held accountable for his actions. Let's start to take care of business, folks.

If we all do this and come together, we can change the way we live for the better. We have got to cut through the red tape so we can all have a better life. If you get a ticket from a cop, I believe that they should just take your driver's license and swipe it through a computer, and you are on your way. It saves tax dollars. The cop doesn't have to take the time to write a ticket, thus the cost of the paper, the time he has to do the paperwork at the station and a few other things are gone.

Let's make as many changes as possible to better ourselves. We owe it to ourselves. If we all come together with stopping at an accident, it would change a lot of things for the better.

Five plus people see what is a set-up accident to claim the insurance. The cop determines with the witnesses' testimony that a possible crime has been committed, and he sends that one to the court for investigation.

If we all do this one thing—come forward and tell the cops who possibly committed a crime—with all the witnesses' testimony, we should be able to cut through the tape and just get to the bottom line. We all saw you do it, and you're guilty.

If *We The People* all come together to show the courts who is good by volunteering, then we can weed out the bad and get rid of them. We would be back to the days where we left our front doors unlocked and our keys in the car and said hi to anyone and got a smile out of them.

Chapter Fourteen

Community Service

Just about everyone who messes up gets community service in their lifetime. But that is just another one of the programs that our government, in my opinion, has not set up properly.

My father taught me that if you are going to do a job, do it right the first time so you don't have to go back and do it right the second time, thus saving you time and money. Are saving time and money on our employees' minds? Consider this:

Say a painter gets community service. He does not go and clean up papers by the highway. He paints some government place and does not pick up trash. A doctor gets community service; he has to do his service at the VA hospital or some other free clinic. A lawyer gets community service and does his time as a public defender instead of picking up trash.

If one of these people decides to not do a good job because they have to do it for free then they will go to jail

If the person who has no skills gets community service, then he or she is the one that picks up trash. Does that make sense? It seems pretty simple to me. A government building needs fixing up, and it costs us, *We The People*, our hard earned money. Well, let's get most of the work done for free, thus lowering our taxes.

Another thing to consider is training prisoners to do all the government fixing up and even new construction. They should be window washers, trash collectors, bathroom cleaners, anything and everything that the government needs doing. The community service people and prisoners should do it all, saving the taxpayer billions of dollars, and also, that would be a program that would really rehabilitate bad people, giving them a trade they could do instead of the crimes that brought them to jail in the first place.

If we sign this petition then the tax payer will save billions of dollars and prisoners will have a chance reentering society.

Chapter Fifteen

Taxes

I hope so far you liked how I showed you how together *We The People* can lower our tax dollars. I know you will love this one. This one petition will save the taxpayer millions of dollars.

Do you know why a shirt in a store costs $12.00 today, and tomorrow it costs $13.50 for the same shirt? It is because the merchant raises the price of the same shirt because they have to recoup their losses of people shoplifting. That's right; *We The People* are paying for the shoplifter's actions.

That is also why, to some extent, our taxes are so high. We have to pay in taxes for the people who don't pay. The government needs so much money to run itself. They have to get it from somewhere, and we're it—those of us who pay taxes. The more people don't pay, the higher our taxes. Well, guess what? I have a solution to that problem as well.

We The People no longer have to pay taxes, that is, on what we earn. We only pay taxes on what we spend. Therefore, everyone will have to pay taxes, thus lowering our taxes. People who do crimes for money will now have to pay taxes on the money they get illegally. I explained my idea to this person, and he said that it wouldn't work because people would not spend their money. Instead, they would barter their services and not pay cash for them, and I believe he is right. But I believe I have a solution to that problem as well.

Take away the piece of paper that says entrapment is illegal, and that petition should just about take care of that problem. You see, you make bartering services illegal and entrapment legal, so by doing that, people won't take a chance because they'll never know. Then someone said, "What about garage sales?" Simple. There are some places of business closed on Saturday and Sunday, and all people wanting to have a sale go to the parking lot. An employee for the government takes their portion, and, in doing so, this plan will create new jobs for people. It will also be good for the sellers because the amount of people showing up for the sale would be great.

When someone sells something in the newspaper or classified ads, the paper collects the money from the buyer, take the taxes out and then give the seller their money. There will be a few changes to some things, but I believe this will better us all. Listen, some people say that we can't pay taxes this way because it won't work, and I say that we need to try because the way that you and I have to pay taxes today isn't working.

Remember, I don't have all the answers to all the problems that we have, but I do have one thing, and that's one mind out of three hundred million people. I came up with all of this, and I know that of some of you who are reading this can improve on any of my ideas. I know that they all can work if *We The People* give them a chance and try to make a difference. Go to my Web site at *www.towethepeople.com* to voice your idea. Let's start to make America what we Americans have been saying to the rest of the world—"how great we are"—and prove it by our actions and not words anymore.

How much more can we do to lower our taxes? As I stated in the last chapter, we get nonviolent criminals to do the work for the government so they do not have to spend that much on construction costs.

You know that if we do this one thing, a lot of good will happen, like rehabilitating criminals. Okay, here's how it will happen. Some guy gets twenty years for something. We teach him a trade so when he gets out, he will have great-paying skills so he can get a job so as not to do the same things that got him to prison in the first place. He'll learn respect and what it takes to be responsible, not just to himself but toward others as well in our community.

You give these guys a chance to get a good-paying job, and they won't want to go back inside. Look, we get basically free labor from prisoners for years doing government building.

You need to sign this petition. Not only will the prisoners thank you, but your friends or family members as well who will no longer be in danger from these people for the simple fact that they want to be good now, now that they have a chance at the American dream. This petition will save all of us millions of dollars and keep a whole lot of us safer in the process.

Chapter Sixteen

Money Down the Drain And Fixing Things That Aren't Broken

I wish, to some degree, that our military were in charge of this government because they are efficient in all they do to some degree. When they go out and do something and something goes wrong, they rewrite the book so that mistake doesn't happen again. Do you think that if our government was run that way we would have the crime that we have today?

I believe we need to fix things before they break, meaning we need to make checkups mandatory. Let's not find out that you are sick and then fix you; let's not wait until you are past the point for fixing and then start to pay money to try. It's called preventive maintenance. For example, this apartment owner hires this plumber to come out to fix a clogged drain time and time again. When the plumber says to the owner, "If you let me just put a little screen in all the sinks to catch the stuff, then you won't have to hire me to come out and unclog the drains, thus saving you money." The apartment owner said no. He wanted to hire the plumber every time there was a clog.

Our government is like the apartment owner. They don't want to look to the future to see what might happen and take care of it now. They just want to wait to see what happens then act accordingly. Should our government do preventive maintenance and take care of things before they break? For example, what is the best choice? (1) When a red light comes on in your car indicating you need oil and you ignore it, what happens? Your motor seizes up and dies. (2) When the red light comes on indicating you need oil, you stop, put the proper amount of oil in the motor, and go on your way.

So which do you think was the best choice, (1) or (2)?

Well, let's look back in history, shall we, and you will see that our government picked the first option. Why? I think because they like spending money rather than saving it when they can. So what do *We The People* do about it?

We vote.

That's right: vote. We vote; we tell our government what to do, and they have to do it. It's that simple. But we have to vote. It is our responsibility. You want a better life? Then you have to vote.

I tell people all the time that I can't fix it if it's not broken. I wish our employees would start doing that as well. It seems to me they waste the taxpayers' money on fixing things that are not broken, like when I was going to junior high school. Well, for those of you who don't know what junior high school is, it's now called intermediate school. What's wrong with junior high and high school?

Why did they waste our money with having to change the name of a school, and how much money did it cost? I don't know, but I do know that money could have been spent on something else worth having done. Why are they putting forth efforts trying to change things that don't need fixing? Is it because *We The People* never told them not to? Or is it because if they don't spend the money in their budget, they won't get it anymore the next year?

There was this other person who wanted to change the color of the scuba divers' flag that they put in the ocean when diving from red and white to blue and white. Do you see a problem here, not in just wasting the taxpayers' money but with the possible harm coming to the scuba diver?

Chapter Seventeen

Iraq War for Sale

This will be another example of how our government knows when people take advantage of it and does nothing about it. The Iraq War is this example.

There are a few different contractors working in Iraq doing various things. In fact, there are over one hundred thousand of them, but for this example they are Halliburton, Blackwater, CACI, KBR, and Titan. Now, I am not making any claims that what I tell you is true; however, I will tell you what the TV said on one of those shows on the Iraq War called *Iraq for Sale*. They claimed that our government hires private contractors to do the jobs that our servicemen already do. Our servicemen are replaced by overpaid private contractors, and they are told to go and stand guard duty somewhere and not do what we trained them for. That alone is proof that our government is corrupted somehow. Why would you pay someone over seven times what you're already getting for less?

This is the petition that I spoke of earlier. Since our government wants to pay more money than they're paying now to private contractors, then we will make it so that our service men and women receive more money than they're receiving now. The average pay that the bulk of our fighting men and women get is between $1,340.40 and $1,750.50 a month. Effective as of January 1, 2008, this petition will increase their pay $1,000.00 a month. As it is right now, the families of these fighting men and women are on food stamps and other subsidized programs because they are not paid enough. They've earned it.

Approximately, 40 percent of every dollar that Congress controls goes to private contractors. But some of that money seems to sneak its way back into the pockets of a couple of congressmen. My question is: why would contractors who do work for the government want to give back money to our Congress? It must be because they overcharged, right?

Well, here's the truth. The top recipients of money from the five named above contractors are the two chairmen of the committees in Congress and the House of Representatives that oversee military matters and spending. Wow, I want a job.

CACI was awarded a contract with no other companies being able to bid on the same.

Halliburton and KBR were awarded contracts without having to bid on them as well.

KBR was awarded seven billion without bidding. Maybe that is why those two chairmen who oversee military matters and spending received money from these companies.

If you are not aware of how our government awards contracts normally, the process is that they put out the word and solicit bids from more than one company, and the lowest bid gets the contract.

A woman named Bunnatine Greenhouse, the former chief contracting officer for the corps of engineers, alleges favoritism and rule breaking. She discovered preferential treatment was given to KBR. They were preselected and were given contracts over all others.

It's bad enough that people are getting kickbacks or whatever today they're calling it. It's another thing that some of these companies who were awarded these contracts didn't even do what that were contracted for, and sickness and death resulted from their actions.

Halliburton was given a contract to give clean water to the military. Of the sixty-seven water treatment plants they were in control of, sixty-three were not providing safe water for your children, and as a result of that, they will be coming home with pathogens in their bodies. For those of you who do not know what a pathogen is, it's an *infectious agent*, or, more commonly, a *"germ,"* a *biological agent* that causes *disease* or *illness* to its *host*. Some pathogens (such as the bacterium *yersinia pestis*, which may have caused the *black plague*, the **variola** virus, and the *malaria* protozoa) have been responsible for massive numbers of casualties and have had numerous effects on afflicted groups. Of particular note in modern times is HIV, which is known to have infected several million humans globally, along with *severe acute respiratory syndrome* (SARS) and the *influenza* virus. Today, while many medical advances have been made to safeguard against infection by pathogens, such as the use of *vaccination, antibiotics,* and *fungicide*, pathogens continue to threaten human life. Social advances such as *food safety, hygiene,* and *water treatment* have reduced the threat from some pathogens.

Sixty-three water-treatment plants were failing, and our government did nothing. Why? Was it because of that god, "the all powerful dollar"? Those whom we trusted with our children said in a loud voice that lining their pockets with the taxpayers' money was more important to them than the lives of those who preserve our freedoms.

According to the evening news, they said that the Pentagon auditory found that Halliburton, who got a contract to feed and house the military, had a staggering $1.8 billion in unsupported costs. Halliburton charged $45.00 per six-pack of Coke they gave to the troops. Halliburton charged $99.00 per load of laundry that would cost under $5.00 here in the States, and most of the uniforms came back unclean due to the fact that the soap that was used was either not soap or the cheapest they could find. The Pentagon auditory found that Halliburton overcharged the military between $150 and $950 million. They were also investigated for overcharging on work already completed to the tune of $450 million.

If this bothers you now, that you now have discovered how our government doesn't care for you or me, then I warn you that what you're about to find out should make you put on sackcloth and ashes.

KBR was in charge of feeding our soldiers and did not to go on a twenty-four-hour feeding schedule that resulted in long lines averaging one hundred personnel, which resulted in the mess hall being filled to capacity. The enemy knew of these times and attacked, killing many personnel. On a twenty-four-hour feeding schedule, no mess halls would have been attacked, saving lives. People died because of greed. KBR didn't go on a twenty-four-hour feeding schedule because it would have cost them more money to do so.

On one particular day, the military contacted Halliburton and a subsidiary of them, KBR, and told them that this certain stretch of highway was under enemy control and under no circumstances should they send any trucks out that day. They were ordered by the military, "Do not go or risk death." I guess money was more important to them than the truck drivers' lives. I don't know how many drivers died that day, but, in my opinion, the ones who sent those drivers out committed murder when they flat-out disregarded the orders from the military not to send anyone.

When you get the bug *greed*, it's hard to shake it off. The contracts that Halliburton and the like receive are called cost plus contracts. Basically, how they work is the more billable items they submit, the more they make.

This type of contracts couldn't be the worst way of ripping off the American people. You shall soon see.

One of the hotels that Halliburton paid for their employees to stay in was fancier than the Ritz or the Four Seasons. They had five-star meals catered in every day.

The military personnel lived in tents without air-conditioning. The tents all had mold, and most personnel contracted respiratory infections. Halliburton supplied tents for our heroes, and for themselves got five-star accommodations.

The transportation that was supplied to the Halliburton employees was forty to eighty thousand dollar vehicles, Hummers and Cadillac Escalades, with all the upgrades you would want on a vehicle from leather seats to CD players. On one lease, they had an SUV that leased out at over $7,000.00 each month for a three-year contract. Its total was somewhere in the range of over $250,000 where you could buy that same SUV for around $45,000.

When Halliburton ordered the wrong equipment, they would throw everything into a pit and light it on fire, claiming a loss. New vehicles and new computers still in the box got burned.

This one person's job was to order things for the sole purpose of burning it so they could make more money. Remember, these are cost plus contracts.

Halliburton had brand-new semi-trucks with no oil filters, and when the motor seized, they bought a new one and billed the government. They had other Semi-trucks that did not have a spare tire, so when they got a flat, they pushed them off the roadway and set them afire. Then they billed the government for a new one. Every day an $80,000 to $100,000 truck broke down for some mysterious reason and then was torched.

Halliburton overcharged our government one billion dollars and still got paid.

Did you know that Dick Cheney was at one point the CEO of Halliburton? It's no wonder they got the contracts and got paid even with all those allegations directed against them. Most of the top officials of Halliburton used to be the top Pentagon officials.

Dick Cheney's office coordinated Halliburton's multibillion dollar deal, and you know what sucks is that our government never ordered a hearing in either the Congress, House, or Senate on their no-bid contracts. The reason no hearings ever took place is because Halliburton donated $3.5 million to the lobbyists, $934,615 to the Political Action Committee (PAC), and $822,901 to the board of directors of some other organization for a total sum of $4,386,000.

CACI/Titan have donated to certain lobbying people $2.2 million, and (PAC) got $617,618 totaling $2.817 million.

Halliburton CEO David Lesar received for his salary $42,637,920 for the year of 2004. Who knows how much more of our taxpayers' money he's getting now.

Halliburton was given contracts that the Iraqi people could have had, even doing a better job in the process, getting them off the streets with a job and not some gun killing our children.

Halliburton and the like are war profiteers, and they should be brought up on charges for murder and embezzling the taxpayers' money and should go to jail for their crimes.

Some of our senators, like Patrick Leahy of Vermont, brought before Congress the amendment that would do just that—make them held accountable for their actions—and it got shot down. Go figure. Ready to vote now?

Chapter Eighteen

Perjury, Adultery, and Sex

How many of you think that if a law is on the books, the law should be enforced? Well, I'm guessing most of you are agreeing with me about enforcing the laws that we have. I mean, why not? Those laws that are on the books now cost the taxpayer money to get them to be laws. Anytime anything comes before our government for consideration it costs us, *We The People*, money. So again, why not enforce them? We paid for them. Might as well use them, right? Here are some examples of laws we have on our books that the government *does not enforce*.

1. *Perjury*. Perjuring oneself before a court of law. People do it all the time with the court's knowledge, and the court doesn't do anything about it. Why? Perjury is against the law, isn't it?
2. *Adultery*. People are caught on tape committing adultery, and the courts don't do anything about it. Why?
3. *Having sex*. The law states that no person is allowed to have sex until they are of legal age, married, or emancipated. Now, come on folks. We know without a shadow of a doubt that when a twelve-year-old girl gets pregnant, she has had sex, right? Did she get busted for having sex? Did the person who got her pregnant got busted also? I don't think so. So since we are not enforcing these laws, take them off the books or start enforcing them.

How many other laws are on the books that no one enforces? You know, what's funny is that our system is kind of like parents raising kids. Yeah, the parent says not to do something, and the child does it anyway. And the parent does not enforce a punishment, so the kid grows up not knowing what responsibility is. When a parent punishes a child who has done something wrong, that child will grow up committing less wrongs than not.

If the courts were to enforce perjury, then that would cause less court time, less tax dollars being spent, and less time for the juror to be on call, which would be all-around better for all. What would happen if they just enforce all laws that are on the books, like people having sex? If a twelve-year-old gets pregnant, she either has to call the police and say she was raped or she goes to jail. Maybe if we start to enforce that law we have on having sex, then maybe there will be fewer pregnancies, fewer abortions, and fewer lives wrecked from our children having sex.

According to the U.S. Centers for Disease Control and Prevention, in the year 2007, 35 percent of U.S. high school students were currently sexually active, and 47.8 percent of U.S. high school students reported having had sexual intercourse.

Some studies have found that engaging in sex leaves adolescents, and especially girls, with higher levels of stress and depression. By the time they are high school seniors, 66 percent of girls and nearly 63 percent of boys report they have had intercourse.

Fact: Over 750,000 kids get pregnant every year from the ages of fifteen to nineteen years old.

Fact: Eight out of ten teen fathers do not marry the mother of their first child.

Fact: The United States has one of the highest rates of teen pregnancy of all developed nations.

Fact: About one-third of girls that get pregnant do it by the age of twenty.

Fact: In the United States, teen mothers are less likely to complete high school and are more likely to live in poverty than other teens.

    These children of ours are getting pregnant and are allowed to get an abortion or keep their child.
    This guy went into a bank, stole $10,000, got caught down the block, and was surprised when the cops told him that he had to give back the money. He said, "What about the law that says 'Possession is nine-tenths of the law?'"
    After five years of marriage, this couple found themselves in court getting a divorce. This woman wanted half of her soon-to-be-ex-husband's wealth and was told that she was not entitled to anything due to the fact that she signed a prenuptial agreement. Well, through the hearings, they discovered that when she signed that prenuptial agreement and when she entered into marriage she was not of legal age, so that agreement was not valid. So she got half of everything that he had.
    My point here in these two examples is that when a minor has sex and wants to give birth or have an abortion, they entered into it illegally, so they also should

not have the rights that someone of legal age has. This petition here will change the lives of so many for the good.

If a minor gets pregnant, she must give birth to the baby, all the while being in juvenile hall, all because she did not call the police telling them she was raped. Then the baby will be put up for adoption, and the parents of the child who gave birth will also lose the right to keep the child's child.

Professor Jane Brown of the University of North Carolina had a five-year, federally funded study showing the more sex kids saw on the TV, the more likely they were to have sex by the age of sixteen.

You take a test before you drive a car; you get tested before you get a job. We get tested all the time for things that we need. We need to have a test that will tell us whether or not we can have children.

These are just three examples of three laws that, if we were to enforce, our tax dollars would be less. Fewer lives would be wrecked, and we would have a lot more happy people out there. If girls did not get pregnant, and I mean children not women, they would not have to grow up too fast, allowing them to stay a kid and keeping them from having to have the responsibility that grown-ups have. This also helps the parents of that *child* not have their lives turned upside down all because the *kid* broke the law. Now, I'm not trying to be a hard-nosed person about all this. I just know what responsibility is because of how my parents raised me, so I think that our government has a responsibility to us, *We The People*, to start doing their job and not change the rules whenever they see fit.

If the law says that something is against the law, then whoever breaks it gets busted, plain and simple. I believe that our courts don't enforce the laws that get broken because it costs too much money to do so, so they don't. I asked a cop once how come the courts don't enforce the laws that are on the books, and he said that it was up to the district attorney to decide which crimes they will pursue and which ones they won't. When asked why they don't go after all of the lawbreakers, they said it's because it costs too much money to go after all of them.

Maybe if we start saving money, then we can enforce all laws.

Remember that judge who got a slap on the wrist and a $100 fine for drunk-driving on his fifth offense? When you, *We The People*, get busted for that crime, we have over $1,200 in fines, alcoholic programs, probation, and even traffic school and maybe even community service. So why shouldn't that judge have all those things happen to him also? Does he not get busted like us because he's better than us? You mean that if one of *We The People* gets a job as one of *We The People's* employees, then instantly they become better than their bosses?

Well, if you don't think it's fair how things work now, then vote and vote today. Sign this petition, and crime will go down.

Who said that there is only a certain time that *We The People* can vote? Do they do that on purpose to keep us controlled? We should be able to vote when someone comes up with something good to vote on. Just like how the military keeps changing their books when needed, the same should be applied on how we get to vote. If in our world something changes, we should change the laws then and not later or not at all in some cases.

If we were to enforce the law of adultery, then maybe fewer families would be wrecked. Maybe the person who was thinking about committing adultery wouldn't because he knew from other people's mistakes that the crime did not outweigh the punishment and he or she knew that if he or she was caught, there would be also jail time involved. Maybe they would get help to save their marriage instead of committing adultery.

For example, a *true story*: this woman never likes to wear a seat belt. She said she didn't want to because it felt uncomfortable, and she wasn't going to wear it. Well, her husband pleaded with her to wear it, and she still refused. Well, she got into a car accident only going about thirty-five miles an hour, and she died. So what happened? Because this woman was selfish, she robbed from her husband a wife; she robbed from her two children a Mom; and she robbed from her whole family and all of her friends. Many people were affected by her choice not to wear a seat belt. She, in my opinion, was a stupid, selfish woman, putting her own needs above everyone else.

I don't ride a motorcycle anymore because of that reason. You see, I weighed riding a bike over not riding one, and my family and friends outweighed my joy for riding. That woman, if she, according to emergency medical services, had worn her seat belt, would only have a bruise on her shoulder and would not have died.

So just like committing adultery, if a person were to weigh how his or her actions would affect others, then maybe that person would make a different decision about having an affair in the first place.

I was watching Judge Judy on TV, and she said something that blew me away. She said that she liked it when both parties in a lawsuit lied. It made her job a little easier. Did the people she catch lying get busted for perjury? When I was watching, Judge Judy asked the plaintiff a question, and the plaintiff lied. Judy asked the plaintiff again the same question and again the same response. When Judge Judy pressured the person, the person came clean. A clear-cut case of perjury, and no one got busted for it. Why?

Judge Milian had a case before her where this man said that he never said over the phone that his wife had a heart attack, and he couldn't show up for work. The plaintiff played a tape recording with him indeed saying what he said he didn't say. Did he get busted for lying? What kind of message does this send to *We The People*? That it's okay to lie before a judge because nothing is going to happen if you do?

My wife laughs that we even have to swear in to tell the truth and nothing but the truth so help us God when lying is proven and nothing happens.

Are the courts saying that God will punish the person and not them? So help you God?

When people lie in court, it does a lot of things, like waste the court's time and cost the taxpayers more money. Let's make our employees start enforcing perjury and busting people for it. Just a thought: maybe if people knew that they would be busted for lying, they would solve their disputes before getting to court. Question: what kind of a world do you think we would live in if people kept the one oath? *I promise to tell the whole truth and nothing but the truth so help me God.* Maybe if the punishment for telling a lie under oath were enforced at a great cost to the liar, then maybe we could help God out of court and lessen his load for all the people lying under oath.

Chapter Nineteen

Thirty-Eight Million

Wow, that's a big number: thirty-eight million. If you were to take the average car at 16 feet and put them front to back, you would need 2,375,000 of them to get to 38 million feet. If you were to carpet one area of the ground, you would need 4,220,480 yards to do so. How about we turn it into money. What could you buy with all that money? Well, if you went to the dollar menu, you could buy thirty-eight million hamburgers, right? Trick question. You would have to use some of that money for tax. But you get the idea, right? You don't need me to tell you what you would buy with $38 million. Okay, what else could we do with thirty-eight million?

Have you ever been to a pro baseball game? Do you remember the first time that you were allowed to go somewhere without supervision? How about hitting your thumb with a hammer? Oh, I know, how about your first kiss?

These were all things that you got to experience. Whether good or bad, it was still something you got to do.

I'll give you another idea of how great a number thirty-eight million is. If you were to turn that thirty-eight into miles, you could go the moon and back one hundred and fifty times.

Another thing that you can do with thirty-eight million is if you were to take a baby and place him or her on the ground, the baby will take up about one square foot, and if you were to place another baby next to the first and so on, you would be able to go around the world about two times. Wow, that's a lot of babies

Imagine having the job of changing all the dirty diapers of those babies that went around the world twice. You would need an army, unless you just let the Mommies and Daddies do it. Wait a minute, that won't happen either, because all those thirty-eight million babies will never get the chance to soil a diaper, go to a ballgame, or even get a chance to get their first kiss, all because back in January 22, 1973, the U.S. Supreme Court legalized unrestricted abortion or, as I like to call it, murder.

Let me give you an example of what our government considers murder to be. I warn you what you are going to read is upsetting at the least and very graphic.

Have you heard of the term "partial-birth abortion"? Well, it goes something like this. With pliers, for lack of a better word for them, the doctor goes up into the woman's body, grabs an arm of a living human being, rips it off the baby, and pulls it out.

Reliable studies have shown that babies suffer excruciating pain when they are killed at twenty weeks gestation and after. Some studies show this even earlier. Oh come on, give me a break. Let me rip your arm off and see if you feel any pain?

So there go the pliers again, coming out with another arm. I wonder if these doctors keep these baby's arms, and when they get enough arms, if they send them off to a furniture store so they can make for themselves an armchair.

Back in go the pliers, and they grab half a leg, rip it off the baby, pull it out, and repeat the process until all that's left is the baby body and head. Now, I am going to assume that the living baby that is being ripped apart literally piece by piece is now dead from bleeding out, and still our government does not at this point consider this to be murder. The baby's heart has stopped beating, and there is no brain function.

The *Uniform Determination of Death Act (UDDA)* is a *uniform act* approved in the *United States* in 1980 by the *National Conference of Commissioners on Uniform State Laws* in cooperation with the *American Medical Association, American Bar Association,* and *President's Commission on Medical Ethics.*

Determination of Death. An individual who has sustained either (1) irreversible cessation of circulatory and respiratory functions, or (2) irreversible cessation of all functions of the entire brain, including the brain stem, is dead. A determination of death must be made in accordance with accepted medical standards.

So we can now assume that the baby is now dead, but for those of you who still believe the baby is still alive, the pliers go back in and grab half the torso and rip it into pieces, spilling all the internal organs into the woman's birth canal. One more time with feeling, the pliers go back inside and take the rest of the baby's body out of the woman, leaving only the head. Putting down the pliers, they pick up a pair of scissors and insert them into the woman's body, jabbing a hole in the back of the baby's head big enough for them to stick a suction hose into the baby's head, sucking out the brains, which results in the baby's head collapsing in on itself.

Okay, all done. The killing and removal of the now-dead baby is complete. What? Oh yeah, the head is still in the woman's body, right? Well, that's done on purpose, and it's up to the woman to push the collapsed head out herself.

Wow, with a capital letter, that's bizaare. Why do they do that, being that the woman has her legs spread and all? Well, that's easy: because if the doctor takes the crushed baby's head out of the woman's birth canal, according to the government, then that would, to them, constitute murder.

Did you like my humor about the armchair? You know what's sad is a lot of you are more disturbed about my lack of sensitivity than the fact that a baby was murdered. Shame on you.

Long-term Complications Associated with Having an Abortion.

- Heavy bleeding (*hemorrhage*).
- Use of RU-486 can also cause *bleeding* which can go on for a month.
- *Cervical laceration* (tearing of the opening to the womb) occurs to 5 percent of women.
- *Puncture or tearing* of the womb (can occur, but go unnoticed and untreated).
- *Infection*—ranges from mild to fatal; sometimes caused by pieces of the baby being left inside the womb.
- If the bleeding is severe enough, or if the puncture in the womb is severe, it may become necessary to remove the uterus (*hysterectomy*).
- Likelihood of *miscarriage is three times greater after an abortion.*
- *Risk of ectopic (tubal) pregnancy increases* by 30 percent after one abortion, 160 percent after two or more abortions; this causes you to lose the baby and your fallopian tube, thereby reducing your chance of conceiving another baby.
- *Premature delivery of future babies* because of damage to the cervix; over three thousand children each year develop *cerebral palsy* because of their premature delivery after the mother's previous abortion.
- *Sterility*—statistics show between one out of fifty to one out of twenty women can never have another baby.
- *Infertility*—caused by scraping that damages the lining of the uterus, leaving scaring that makes it difficult to get pregnant again.
- *Breast cancer*—a National Cancer Institute study found a 50 percent increased risk of breast cancer among eighteen hundred women who had abortions. The risk was doubled for those women whose abortion took place before age eighteen or over age thirty. The majority of studies uphold these results.
- *Psychological disturbances*, including feelings of guilt, depression, feelings of detachment from others, increased drug or alcohol abuse, nightmares and flashbacks, decreased maternal bonding, insomnia, and suicidal thoughts. These can occur years after the abortion.

So to not be accused of not giving you all the information on how the doctors can kill a baby, these are the rest of the ways a woman can have an abortion:

- *Dilation and Evacuation (D and E):* Similar to a D and C abortion. The child is larger and must be dismembered by a curette; also, the head is crushed and removed by forceps. Primarily used on the thirteen-to-twenty-week-old baby.
- *Saline Solution:* This is a less popular method at this time. A concentrated salt solution is injected into the amniotic fluid surrounding the baby. The baby swallows and inhales this solution and dies one to two hours later from poisoning, dehydration, hemorrhaging of internal organs, and convulsions. The mother then goes into labor and delivers a dead or dying baby.
- *Prostaglandin Abortion:* Hormones are given that induce labor, and the mother goes into a labor that is usually violent and very painful because of the high concentrations of the hormone. Not used much because of the danger of delivering a live baby.
- *Hysterectomy:* An early C-section is performed, usually after the baby has been killed by brain aspiration, intercardiac injection (causes the baby to have a heart attack), or cutting the umbilical cord and allowing the baby to bleed to death.
- *Intercardiac Injection:* An ultrasound is used to locate the baby's heart. Fluid is then injected into the heart, causing a heart attack, and killing the preborn baby. Used in hysterectomy abortions: also commonly used when multiple babies are present in order to kill a few that the others may have a better chance of living or when a baby is "defective" in some way.

Fact: Approximately 90 percent or more of couples who have an abortion end their relationship with each other.

Reasons for Abortions

In 2000, cases of rape or incest accounted for 1 percent of abortions. Another study, in 1998, revealed that women reported the following reasons for choosing an abortion:

- 25.5 percent: Want to postpone childbearing
- 21.3 percent: Cannot afford a *baby*
- 14.1 percent: Has relationship problem or partner does not want pregnancy
- 12.2 percent: Too young; parent(s) or other(s) object to pregnancy
- 10.8 percent: Having a *child* will disrupt *education* or *job*

- 7.9 percent: Want no (more) *children*
- 3.3 percent: Risk to *fetal* health
- 2.8 percent: Risk to *maternal* health
- 2.1 percent: Other

According to a 1987 study that included specific data about *late abortions* (i.e. abortions "at 16 or more weeks' gestation"), women reported that various reasons contributed to their having a late abortion:

- 71 percent: Woman didn't recognize she was pregnant or misjudged gestation
- 48 percent: Woman found it hard to make arrangements for abortion
- 33 percent: Woman was afraid to tell her partner or parents
- 24 percent: Woman took time to decide to have an abortion
- 8 percent: Woman waited for her relationship to change
- 8 percent: Someone pressured woman not to have abortion
- 6 percent: Something changed after woman became pregnant
- 6 percent: Woman didn't know timing is important
- 5 percent: Woman didn't know she could get an abortion
- 2 percent: A fetal problem was diagnosed late in pregnancy
- 11 percent: Other

I hope you sign this petition for those who cannot speak for themselves. Our leaders cannot agree on when a baby is considered a human being and has rights, so this petition will fix all of that forever. When the egg splits into two, life is formed and thus should be protected.

What would you do if you had a magic lamp with a genie in it? Would you rub it? Why? Well, that's easy: because you want something. Well, guess what? I am going to be that genie for you if I can get support from others. This is what I propose: if you get pregnant, do not get an abortion, and we will put your child up for adoption, then I will give you what you want. Want a new car or go to college? I will pay for you to get what you want if you qualify and are willing to go through counseling, schooling, and diet restrictions and exercise.

Chapter Twenty

God is I Am

I brought up God just now to give him his day in court. I asked you a couple of times why this nation is the greatest country in the world. So I ask again—why? It is because of one thing. Join in when you know the words.

"I pledge allegiance to the flag of the United States of America and to the Republic for which it stands, one nation under God, indivisible, with liberty and justice for all."

Did you catch which part of that phrase is why we are the greatest nation on earth? *One nation under God.* All of our forefathers were God-fearing men and knew that a nation that was ruled by men and not God would fall. So they put their faith in God and let Him do the ruling, not themselves.

When our forefathers started this country, they, for the most part, believed in God and wanted to obey him, according to his rules. That's how we got the U.S. Constitution; they took the principles from the Bible and drafted up that document.

A long time ago, this ruler of a country said to his servant, "Go and see why the United States was the greatest country in the world." So he came here and looked at our schools and found nothing special. It was the same as where he came from. So he decided to look at our industry to see if that was the reason why the United States was so strong, and again it was basically the same as his. So he decided to see if the reason was because of the military and again the same thing. Puzzled and bewildered, not knowing why we were so great, he decided to check out church, it being Sunday and all. There he found his answer. So he left, and when he got home, his ruler asked him what he found and asked if it was because of industry. The servant said no. "Is it because of their schools?" The servant said quietly—no. "Then it's got to be because of the great military, right?" The servant said no. "Then what's the reason?" The servant said, "Because the United States is one nation under God, meaning that the people living in the United States all just about believed in God, thus having the *ability to govern themselves.*"

Believing in God and governing oneself go hand in hand. I'll show you what I mean.

Can anyone reading this tell me what the safest town to live in in the United States is? Well, I'm not going to tell you. But I will tell you why. You see, there in that town is a Christian college, and 85 percent of the population that lives in that town has some connection with that college. 85 percent or more of the population in that town believe in God and say they love God because *God said that if you truly love me that you would do all that I say,* and I guess they do because of all the towns in the United States, this one has the least crime rate of them all. See what happens when we govern ourselves? Well, since most of the criminals refuse to govern themselves, we have to make the punishment great so the people will have to govern themselves. If we make the punishment great, then there will be less crime. In some other countries, if you steal a loaf of bread, they cut off your hand. In another country, if they catch you stealing, they kill you. Well, I'm not saying that is the punishment we should enforce, but if we make it tough, you know, kind of a deterrent, maybe there would be less crime.

For example, we should make doing drugs legal, but make drug dealing an offense punishable by death. And that should just about end the drug problem. You see, drug users are really not the problem; it's the dealers. Or is the problem with drugs this country's facing the government's fault? Rumor has it that our government likes the drug problem we're facing because it makes them a lot of money. They get to build more prisons, hire more police officers, *etc.* There are billions of dollars being made by illegal drugs.

Do you really think that they want the illegal drug use to end? Don't you think that if they really wanted to, they could end this problem?

The drug user has a disease and can't help him or herself, but the drug dealer is only in it for the money. So if you did make the offense that strong, there would be, by force, a lot of sober people out there.

There was something major that happened back in 1963. Can you guess what that was? That was when the Supreme Court said that it wasn't constitutional to keep the Ten Commandments in public view in court buildings and schools, and when asked why they took it down, the response was that the Ten Commandments might influence someone.

Chapter Twenty-One

Welfare is not fair

Some people who want to work can't find work; therefore, the ones who try to find work should get welfare, not the people who want to stay home eating popcorn and watching TV. I don't want my tax dollars to go to them anymore. How about you? These people take advantage of the system thinking they can just skate by. It's not fair, so I think those who do not try to find work, our employees, and the government, should make them work for their welfare. But how to do it?

One welfare recipient I know says that because she has kids and has no experience at anything, she can only get a job at minimum wage. With the amount of money she makes, she would not be able to afford a babysitter. Therefore, she can't work and needs to get welfare to get by.

There are two solutions. One is she gets a job at minimum wage and welfare pays the difference so she can get by that way, or solution number two is that some other welfare recipient who lives in her area will baby-sit for her so she can go out and get a job and get off welfare. By doing this, the welfare department wouldn't have to pay all the money they now have to spend for all the people on welfare, saving us, the taxpayer, more money.

> *You want welfare—you work for it.*
> *But no one gets money for free,*
> *as it was in the days of old.*

You sign this petition, and a few good things will happen. We all know that when you get anything for free, it doesn't mean anything, but if you work hard and get a paycheck, that does something to you. It makes you respect yourself and those around you for the same reason: you earned it. It will also lower the taxpayers' money that they have to pay now.

Chapter Twenty-Two

Blah, Blah, Blah, and Your Vote

Again folks, it's all up to you—*please vote*. Here's another reason why *We The People* need to vote now, and it's because of a movie that came out a few years ago. It was called *Deep Impact*, yet according to the newspapers, people are calling it the feel-good movie of the summer. Why? It is because a big rock from outer space took out Washington D.C. Kind of sad, wouldn't you say? We have gotten to a point where *We The People* really need to change things, if that's how we really think of our employees the government. Do you know what the Declaration of Independence says about this problem we're facing?

This is part of what the Declaration of Independence says:

> "We hold these truths to be self-evident, that all men are created equal, that they are endowed by their Creator with certain unalienable Rights, that among these are Life, Liberty and the pursuit of Happiness. That to secure these rights, Governments are instituted among Men, deriving their just Powers from the consent of the governed,—*That whenever any Form of Government becomes destructive of these ends, it is the Right of the People to alter or to abolish it, and to institute new Government, laying its foundation on such principles and organizing its powers in such form*, as to them shall seem most likely to effect their Safety and Happiness. Prudence, indeed, will dictate that Governments long established should not be changed for light and transient causes; and accordingly all experience hath shewn, that mankind are more disposed to suffer, while evils are sufferable, than to right themselves by abolishing the forms to which they are accustomed. But when a long train of abuses and usurpations, pursuing invariably the same Object evinces a design to reduce them under absolute Despotism, *it is their right, it is their duty, to throw off such Government, and to provide new guards for their future security*[.]"

*I want **We The People** to alter our government
according to these writings.*

Have we let our government go too far? Can we fix all the wrongs that have been committed?

Do we even want to try? Well, you know what? I don't think we have a choice because if we don't, *God help us.*

All I ever hear is people talking, but no one is doing anything about it. Well, here is your chance. *We The People* come together for once and make good things happen. Here is our chance to put up or shut up. I hope we do something rather than not.

You know it is all about being fair and equal, everyone having the same opportunities as everyone else, and if we stop complaining about how bad things have gotten and start making things better, our grandkids will grow up in a country that our forefathers wanted it to be in the first place, *united*. For we are the United States, remember? Let's act like it, shall we? So have I convinced you to vote or do you need some more convincing? Should I have to try to convince you to vote, or is it really your duty to vote? Because the truth is, one vote really makes a difference.

In the *Citizen's News*, Paul Harvey states, "that in 1948 just one additional vote in each precinct would have elected Dewey." In 1960, one vote in each precinct in Illinois would have elected Nixon—just one vote.

In 1844, a man was not going to vote because he was going to have a big day at work and wanted to get a good start on the day when a friend stopped him on his way to work and got him to vote. Guess what happened? The guy he voted for won by the margin of one vote—his. You see, that one person made a difference by voting. Do you want to make a difference? Then vote.

Do you still believe that your vote won't make a difference? Well, Thomas Jefferson was elected president by just one vote and so was John Quincy Adams. One vote gave statehood to California, Idaho, Oregon, Texas, and Washington. Also, by just one vote the draft act of World War II passed. *Just one vote*. Now, I know that if you do vote, there is no way for you to know if it was your vote that made the difference, but I know that if we all vote and we all agree on something, then you can have the knowledge that your vote counted. In Paul Harvey's writings, Edmund Burke (a wise man, in my opinion), *said, "all that is necessary for the forces of evil to win in this world is for the good people to do nothing."* Well, not voting is doing nothing. So please don't do nothing. Please vote.

Don't allow the bad people to take away from us the very thing that we, as a people, have gotten by our lives in the past ten wars at the point of a gun to be taken away one vote at a time. You see the bad people in our government, and, again, they're not all bad. They vote and laws are made with us, *We The People*, not knowing they did it.

Have you heard of the voting system called the "Electoral College Vote"? Well, in its time it was a great thing. But it is not needed anymore. Our forefathers knew that the people they were trying to govern over were just simple farmers not really privy to what they wanted to do, so they came up with this type of voting system because the average person was not well-informed about the whole thing that they wanted to do. Well, guess what?

We The People are now well-informed and are, for the most part, not illiterate, so that type of voting is not needed anymore. We need to make voting one person, one vote. Count the votes, and find a winner. Can you see the possibility here? If we all vote, what can happen? Did you know that in the Philippines when they vote they get a turnout of at least 93 percent of the population? In our country, not even half voted that were eligible, and you wonder why we are in the mess we are in.

President Kennedy said, "It's not what your country can do for you, it's what you can do for your country." You can vote for the sake of your country. Vote, and we will have a better place to live. Question—how many of you, if given the opportunity to keep ten pounds of gold if you could carry it for ten miles without dropping it, would do it? I think just about everyone would be lining up to try. Now, wouldn't you also agree that after a few miles, the ten pounds of gold would easily feel like one hundred pounds and maybe by the tenth mile you would be in agony? But you would keep suffering because you knew you would be a lot better off with that ten pounds of gold than not. My point is if we put our petty differences aside, all that we try to do in the long run will benefit us all. We just have to try, and that is the key thing here. We try until it all works, but we don't give up.

A man named William C. Kohler wrote

"Tribute to the Flag."

"I rode with Ethan Allen and the Green Mountain Boys. I saw the signal in Boston's Old North Church that started the midnight ride of Paul Revere. I was flown above the decks of 'Old Ironsides,' and from the masts of the 'Yankee' and the 'China Clippers.' I blazed the westward trail with Daniel Boone and Davy Crockett. I led the settlers going west and crossed Death Valley in a covered wagon.

"I was carried through 'the Halls of Montezuma and to the shores of Tripoli' by the United States Marine Corps. I once fell to the ground at Custer's Last Stand, and there were no living hands left to pick me up. I galloped up the slopes of San Juan Hill with Colonel Teddy Roosevelt and the Rough Riders of the United States Cavalry. I stayed with the boys until it was over. Over there, on the battlefields of the Marne, Chateau Thierry, St. Mihiel, and the Argonne forest.

"I saw many of the youth and manhood of our nation fall and lie still in death. They had given their last full measure of blood and devotion. The war was over for them forever, but I kept my lonely vigil over their graves and stayed to watch the poppies grow amid their crosses, row on row, in Flanders Field. I was raised by five brave marines and sailors during the hell of Iwo Jima during World War II. I waved farewell to the four immortal chaplains who went down with their ship to honored glory.

"*I am many things to many people, and I am an inseparable link in the chain that binds men to God and country—each link welded in the fires of purity by the sacred hand of God himself—and because I am on the side of God, the godless would destroy me.* But they dare not, because I am protected by the mighty land armies of our nation, the powerful and deadly fleet of our Navy, and the screaming eagles of our Air Force, watching and waiting to swoop down and destroy anything that would harm me.

"I have not changed much in over two hundred years. I still have my original thirteen stripes, but as each state came into the union, a new star was proudly added to the constellation of my blue field. It started with thirteen stars, for the original thirteen colonies. Now there are fifty.

"I draped the caskets of our nation's heroes and bore to their last resting place the caskets of presidents, generals, admirals, humble privates, and the unknown soldier. Wherever free men gather, wherever there is *justice, equality, faith, hope, charity, truth and brotherly love*, there, too, am I.

"The next time you stand with your hand over your heart and recite the Pledge of Allegiance to me, don't merely mouth the words, but think of what they mean to you and mean what you say. And when you come to the phrase '*One Nation Under God*,' remember that it matters not what your religious beliefs are, *it only matters that you hold your faith dear and that you practice it daily, and preserve it forever.*

"History will never write my obituary; for I am the stars and stripes forever… *I am 'Old Glory.' I am your flag! I am you!!*"

So I will ask you again, do you want to vote, or does anything you have read mean anything to you?

You know, too many people these days only talk, and it seems no one does anything about anything. So here is our chance to do something good for our most great nation: we vote.

We vote, and great things will happen. Our kids will grow up saying what a great job their mothers and fathers did to create a great nation for them. This petition we need to sign. We need to make it mandatory that everyone votes. Besides, we owe it to the ones who came before us who gave their lives to preserve this freedom to make our voice known.

Chapter Twenty-Three

The Draft

Going to school is a great thing. The school teaches us how to live on our own when we graduate so we can move out of our parent's house and make a life for ourselves. But you know what? Our schools don't teach our children respect and responsibility. Guess who does? The military does. You go in a kid and come out an adult, knowing what responsibility is, knowing what teamwork is and how to get along and work with others.

School teaches you how to live on your own; the military teaches you the rest. So should not all kids that graduate from school go into boot camp for six months? Now, I know a lot of the kids will complain and not want to go, but hey, we made them go to school for eighteen years, what's six months more, right? If we did this, other things would happen as well. For one thing, there would be less crime out there, again saving the taxpayer more money.

There would be no more commercials for the military on TV soliciting people to join, thus saving the taxpayer more money, and this would also fill a need our military is facing—good people. Yes, that's right. You see, people sign up to go in the military and within the first six weeks of boot camp they know they made a mistake and want out but are stuck for the next two to four years that they signed up for. So what do we have? We have a person defending our country not giving it their 100 percent, but there are some people who sign up and love it. They make a career out of it. The ones who like their job will do a better job than the one who hates his job, right? So if we make it mandatory, we will get the ones who want that kind of life, thus protecting us better, and the least that can happen is the ones who don't want that type of life will come out of boot camp having learned respect, honor, and discipline.

The draft is a device with which our government picks out of a lottery who will fight and defend our country in case of war. So with six months of training behind them, they stand a better chance of living through a war than not having that extra training. I know that there are a lot of single parents out there, and I know that they can't teach their kids everything they want to teach because their kid is rebellious. So let's let the military help us do this.

Sign this petition, and this one will save lives, maybe even one of yours.

Chapter Twenty-Four

Presidential Executive Orders

Do you like the Constitution and the Bill of Rights because of what they do for you? Well, guess what. There is a law that is on our books right now that will suspend the Constitution and the Bill of Rights with no way of reinstating it. Did you know that? Do you care? Well, our future is in all of your hands, *We The People*. It's all up to you. What are you going to do about it? I'm hoping you will vote. Laws that are on the books got there because of what is called a Presidential Executive Order.

A Presidential Executive Order is a law that our president can make up, no matter how stupid or horrific it may be, without the knowledge of the Senate or Congress, and it becomes law and will be upheld. Congress can disapprove any executive order during the customary thirty-day period in order to prevent it from becoming law. They have only done that three times that I know of.

Our forefathers clearly wanted to have nothing to do with the kind of despotic control that is associated with a royal ruling class such as a king or a dictatorship, so they established a republic to achieve that. Authority was divided among three branches of government to provide checks and balances and avoid an inordinate concentration of power in any one branch.

In light of this history, the Presidential Executive Order could facilitate a form of dictatorial rule. Executive orders have a worthwhile purpose when correctly applied, but their use has been corrupted over time, oftentimes for political gain.

Because of the Executive Orders that are on the books now, what you're about to read is not so farfetched. If you do not vote then the life you have now will not be yours anymore to do what you want. There will be no more sporting events to go to or watch on TV, no more movies will be made for you to be entertained, you will not have any more parties at your home and you will not get to purchase whatever you want whenever you want. There will be no more celebrating any holidays including Christmas. No more water or snow skiing and for that matter you will no longer be able to do anything for fun. Now I can sit here and tell all the thing that you will not be able to do but I will let your own imagination figure it out.

Pretend for a moment that you are relaxing in your home watching TV just after dinner when suddenly there's a knock on the door. When you answer the door, you are abruptly seized, ripped from your home, stripped of your private property, and carried away against your will to a concentration camp where you are held prisoner.

Where have you heard of something like this happening? Nazi Germany? How about here in our country? It happened in 1942 to over one hundred thousand of our own citizens. This happened without public debate. This happened without Congress's approval. All that was required was a simple signature of the president. Over one hundred thousand American citizens' lives were turned upside down, all because of the Presidential Executive Order.

In 1933, at the request of President Roosevelt, the U.S. Congress passed the *War and Emergency Powers Act*, which has never been repealed. This legislation was an amendment to the *Trading with the Enemies Act*, which was originally passed by Congress in 1917.

Due to the circumstances surrounding World War I, the president was granted full authoritarian control of citizens of enemy countries who were living or working in this country and of their property.

This act expressly excluded domestic transactions; that is, those being conducted by American citizens. The amended 1933 version effectively reclassified U.S. citizens within the "enemy" category. At this point, U.S. citizens were made enemies of the federal government

President Franklin Delano Roosevelt provided his name, which was the instrument he used to create Executive Order 9066 of the Constitution.

Our forefathers knew that without the kind of government that they wanted to create, that scenario above could happen. It is doubtful that the forefathers ever envisioned a president having the ability to create law without even the semblance of representative government. Yet here we are today.

The U.S. Constitution is absolutely clear without any ambiguity whatsoever in the fact that only Congress has the exclusive right to enact all law.

Article I, Section 1. "*All legislative Powers* herein granted shall be *vested in a Congress* of the United States, which shall consist of a Senate and House of Representatives."

I pray that after reading these Orders, you will become so outraged that you will get involved and sign all these petitions so that we all can return our country back *To We The People*.

The Presidential Executive Order 11051 gives a detailed plan how all the other Presidential Executive Orders will be orchestrated into effect.

Executive Order 10995 provides for the takeover of the communications media.

Executive Order 10997 provides for the takeover of all electric power, petroleum, gas, fuels, and minerals.

Executive Order 10999 provides for the takeover of all modes of transportation, control of highways, seaports, etc.

Executive Order 11000 provides for mobilization of all civilians into work brigades under government supervision.

Executive Order 11001 provides for governmental takeover of all health, education, and welfare functions.

Executive Order 11002 designates the postmaster general to operate a national registration of all persons.

Executive Order 11003 provides for the government to take over airports and aircraft.

Executive Order 11004 provides for the housing and finance authority to relocate communities, designate areas to be abandoned, and establish new locations for populations.

Executive Order 11005 provides for the government to take over railroads, inland waterways, and public storage facilities.

Question: why are all these Executive Orders, plus much more, on our books? Is it because our government has a plan to do something? Are you scared enough now to vote? For all of this to come into effect is for our president to declare a national emergency, and the organization called FEMA will take over and implement all orders.

FEMA is the *Federal Emergency Management Agency*.
FEMA itself came into existence by means of an executive order.

An emergency is defined by federal law as "any occasion or instance for which, in the determination of the President, federal assistance is needed to supplement state and local efforts and capabilities to save lives and to protect property and public health and safety, or to lessen or avert the threat of a catastrophe in any part of the United States."

Question: if all these Executive Orders go into effect, what will happen to our country? What will the new name of our country be, since we will have thrown out the Constitution and Bill of Rights? Where will we be then? I know we will no longer be free or united. So do you want to vote now?

Go to your computer and type in this link if you want to get the "you know what" scared out of you: *http://maps.google.com/maps/ms?hl=en&gl=us&ie=UTF8 &oe=UTF8&msa=0&msid=118135173934136151745.00045bc25ee928a8872d0*

After you do this, watch the You Tube video.

Okay, one more thing to vote on, and that is "Who are you going to vote for president the next time you have a chance to do it?" Do you want a president with an agenda set forth before you in this writing, a man who wants to fix things when they break, leave things alone if they aren't broken, and think of ways to keep our country united? Or do you want another person with a hidden agenda being your president?

My name is Christopher Ben Largey.
Thank you.

My Mission Statement

What I want to do for my family and yours is get your votes, take them to Washington, present them to our leaders, and tell them to make these things that you and I have stated that we want done to become a reality.

I want to be a *watchdog* for *We The People*, keep an eye on our employees and report back who is doing their job and who isn't. This will cost a lot of money to keep all of *We The People* informed, so I'm asking you to help spread the word. Tell your friends to get a book for this cause. We need all of *We The People* to join together to make the ideas in this book work.

I want a better place to live. To live without fear, I want to know that if I get sick, I will be cared for. I want my government run by *We The People*, not people with hidden agendas.

On the following pages is where you will vote, and then mail them back to me so I can take them with me to Washington.

If you have any other family members that are at least eighteen years old or older, photocopy the forms and send them all in together with whatever else you want to the address below.

Send all votes and correspondence to:
Christopher Largey
270 E. Hunt Highway Suite 16 # 244
San Tan Valley AZ 85143

Put a check mark in the boxes that you want to vote on, and put a pencil line through the ones that you don't want to vote on.

I'm not saying that any or all of these things that we vote on here will ever become law. But what I am saying is that if you send in your vote on these forms, it will show our government that *We The People* are saying that enough is enough and that we want them all to start doing their jobs and to start fixing the things that need fixing.

Dear employees, my government,   Date _____
To whom it may concern.
My name is _____

Address
_____

City, State, Zip
_____

I vote is the boxes check marked and that you make them happen, so help you!

- ☐ I say feed the hungry.
- ☐ I say allow *We The People* to sign away our rights like the government does when they want to.
- ☐ I say do not allow the Federal Drug Administration people to be able to hold any stocks in any pharmaceutical companies.
- ☐ I say we advertise on government property, like on the back of the freeway signs and on stamps.
- ☐ I say all lottery money goes to the schools.
- ☐ I say we charge $5.00 for each person who visits the United States.
- ☐ I say we tax $0.02 each time we talk on the telephone to help pay off the deficit.
- ☐ I say we pay $0.01 extra per gallon to help pay off the deficit.
- ☐ I say we ticket ourselves with a transponder.
- ☐ I say we get brownie points for being good.
- ☐ I say all cars should have a shut off switch that the police can throw to stop a suspect from fleeing, saving lives in the process.
- ☐ I say we allow the military to become self-supportive.
- ☐ I say we all sign up for the same health insurance so we can pay $20.00 per month for full coverage.
- ☐ I say we make voting mandatory.
- ☐ I say we need to simplify and make sure everyone understands all measures being voted upon via the computer.
- ☐ I say we should make all candidates have the same opportunities and share in all the campaign contributions.
- ☐ I say we hold all civil officers accountable for their actions.
- ☐ I say we start impeachment for employees who are not doing their jobs.
- ☐ I say we make all judges accountable for their actions.
- ☐ I say we let vets who have seen war go to any hospital.

To We The People

- ☐ I say vets should get $1,000 per month extra up to pay grade 4.
- ☐ I say vets do not have to pay taxes again, unless they make over $55,000 per year.
- ☐ I say we make prisons be self-supportive.
- ☐ I say make two sets of rules for all of us, one for good people and one for bad.
- ☐ I say we make two sets of prisons, one for good people and one for bad.
- ☐ I say that most of the people who get arrested for doing drugs get house arrest.
- ☐ I say all criminals get all their rights taken away from them until they can earn them back.
- ☐ I say we use prisoners to pick the food in the field.
- ☐ I say we use prisoners to do the construction for most of the government.
- ☐ I say we deport anyone who is in our country illegally.
- ☐ I say we should mine our borders with bombs.
- ☐ I say we use the $338 billion spent on illegal aliens and give it to social security.
- ☐ I say we give tax credits or brownie points to people who give blood to the Red Cross.
- ☐ I say a person who gets in an accident gets three times the doctor bill for pain and suffering and the cost to fix the vehicle.
- ☐ I say cops should just swipe your driver's license, and you are on your way when you get a ticket.
- ☐ I say that people who get community service should use their talents for the good of the government, and if they do not have any skills, they will clean up our roads.
- ☐ I say we should pay taxes on what we spend and not on what we earn.
- ☐ I say we should make entrapment legal in certain cases.
- ☐ I say we make garage sales only on government land like school parking lots or the DMV, etc.
- ☐ I say we make medical checkup mandatory for all people.
- ☐ I say we allow the government agencies to get the same amount of money each year, even if they haven't used up their allotted amount of money for that year.
- ☐ I say that all people who have committed crimes in the Iraq war should be brought up on charges for their crimes.
- ☐ I say that we impeach the two chairpeople of the Appropriation Committee and start going down the list and getting them all.
- ☐ I say that we go through the books and get rid of all the laws that don't apply today.

- ❑ I say we make all laws that we have on the books today enforced.
- ❑ I say if a minor gets pregnant, she must give birth to the baby all the while being in juvenile hall, unless she was raped.
- ❑ I say if a girl gets pregnant and does not call the police, she must go to juvenile hall.
- ❑ I say if a girl has sex with a boy, the boy must go to juvenile hall as well.
- ❑ I say that no parents of the child will be entitled to adopt the baby.
- ❑ I say that no child has the right to have an abortion, due to the fact that they entered into an illegal act.
- ❑ I say we make people take a test to see if they should have children or not.
- ❑ I say we should be able to vote once a month when new things come up and not wait every two to four years to do so.
- ❑ I say when an egg splits in the woman's womb, life starts and should be protected.
- ❑ I say we should make the punishment for crimes tougher so as to lessen crime.
- ❑ I say we put the Ten Commandments back on the walls of our schools and government buildings.
- ❑ I say we make it necessary for all children who graduate high school to go into the military for six months.
- ❑ I say people who get welfare should work for it.
- ❑ I say we start to impeach all of our representatives who are now eligible for impeachment if they do not start doing their *job*.
- ❑ I say that we should do away with the Electoral College voting system and get back to one vote, one person to see who wins.
- ❑ I say that we end the pay scale that Congress now makes when they retire.
- ❑ I say we throw off such a government and get a new one.

Signed this _____ day of _____ 2009
X _____